Praise for Iraqi Jews: A History of Mass Exodus

'This is a good, brief and well-documented account of the exodus of the Iraqi Jews.'

Charles Glass, *Spectator*

'Shiblak's excellently researched and referenced work looks behind the tragedy. He carefully demonstrates the strains which the creation of an Israeli state imposed on the Iraqi Jews.'

Simon Taggart, *Tribune*

'Shiblak's account is extremely honest, carefully researched and well documented.'

Simone Bitton, *Etudes Palestiniennes*

'Shiblak's analysis is fair-minded and well balanced. It is a solid work of scholarship based on much research in primary sources.'

Nissim Rejwan, *Jerusalem Post*

'Shiblak's book is especially important. It is well researched and documented. He treats with sympathy the last days of a prosperous, industrious and conscientious community.'

Meer Basri, *Jewish Quarterly*

'Shiblak tackles the still controversial issue of Iraqi Jewish emigration with skill and objectivity. His book will stimulate anyone trying to piece together the complex issue of communal co-existence in the Arab world.'

Susan Willock, *Middle East International*

'One cannot fail to appreciate the skill, care and objectivity with which Shiblak presents his analysis and conclusions.'

Khalid Qishtainy, *Arab Affairs Quarterly*

'Shiblak has produced a book of great significance to anyone wanting to understand the disruption and chaos caused by the Zionist scheme in the Middle East, not only amongst Arabs but also amongst the Jews themselves.'

Sara Saleem, *Arabia*

'Shiblak's book is a powerful and most convincing account of the exodus of the Iraqi Jews.'

al-Majallah

'Reading Shlomo Hillel on Iraqi Jews is like watching Rambo who is fond of himself and his dubious achievements. Reading Shiblak, one gains a realistic understanding of the circumstances that led to the exodus of this prosperous and deep-rooted community.'

Jihad al-Khazen, *al-Yum*

'The book is a landmark in the history of the Iraqi Jews after decades of silence and deceit.'

Adel Samara, *al-Arab*

Abbas Shiblak

IRAQI JEWS

A History of Mass Exodus

Preface by
Peter Sluglett

SAQI

British Library Cataloguing-in-Publication Data
A catalogue record for this book is available from the British Library

ISBN 0 86356 504 2
Ean 9-780863-565045

First published as
The Lure of Zion, London 1986
This edition published 2005

SAQI
26 Westbourne Grove
London W2 5RH
www.saqibooks.com

To the memory of Dawood Cohen

Contents

Tables

9

Appendices

Acknowledgements

I am extremely grateful to Sami Daniel, mentor and colleague, and Bob Sutcliff, both of Kingston University, and Sami Zubaida of Birkbeck College, University of London, for their advice and valuable comments and to Roger Owen of St Antony's College, Oxford University, for his initial encouragement and help while preparing this book.

I have benefited from discussions with several members of the Iraqi Jewish community about their recollections of life in Iraq and their help is gratefully acknowledged. These include: Yacoub, Heskeel and Habiba Kojman, Clair Cohen, Munir Shaby and Me'ir Basri, the last president of the Iraqi Jewish community, and the late Ahmad Sosa, who converted to Islam at an early stage and stayed in Baghdad with his family. None of these are in any way responsible for the views expressed in this book.

Helpful advice on Arabic sources was received from Sulafa al-Hajjawi of the Iraqi National Archive and Samira al-Mani' in London. Amina and Elias Nasr-Allah, Athil Kojman and Haqi Cohen helped with Hebrew sources. I am grateful to them all. I am also grateful to Nur Masalha and Yehouda Shenhav. Their recent works based on new Israeli archive documents greatly helped in filling gaps from the first edition of this book that I felt needed to be addressed. Special thanks goes to Heather Allen and Lucine Taminian for reading the draft manuscript and suggesting numerous stylistic improvements. My gratitude also extends to my son Rami who helped in proof reading. My wife Farihan was most understanding and supportive during the period of preparation of the original manuscript.

Preface

Peter Sluglett

One rainy evening in the early 1980s, my wife and I paid our first visit to Abbas Shiblak at his home in North London. 'Let's go and see some Iraqi friends', he said. We drove about twenty minutes, and stopped outside a semi-detached house in a quiet neighbourhood. When we entered the house, about ten people greeted us, and we were soon sitting in a semi-circle in the living room, drinking arak. The evening went on; people talked, we ate an Iraqi meal; someone brought out an *'ud*, and all the men began to sing Iraqi *maqamat*.

At that stage I did not know Abbas well, and had only the vaguest idea about the thesis he was planning to write. If I had known him better, it might have dawned on me rather more quickly than it eventually did that everyone in the room except for the guests had been connected in some way to the Iraqi Communist Party, and that all the Iraqis were Jewish. They had all been obliged to leave Iraq at various different times, often having served long sentences in Iraqi jails both before and after the Revolution of 1958; they had all gone to Israel, where one of them had been a member of the Knesset. One by one they decided they could stand Israel no longer, and, because they could, they had found their way to London. Of course they could not go back to Iraq, for a different combination of the reasons which have kept Abbas from returning to Haifa, except, of course, in his incarnation as a British tourist. So there they were, the Iraqi Jews who felt themselves so alien and out of place in

13

Israel that they had felt obliged to leave, with their Palestinian Muslim friend who also found himself in London, unable to return to the land from which he and his family had fled in 1948.

It is a great pleasure to introduce a new edition of *Iraqi Jews: A History of Mass Exodus*, the definitive account of the expulsion of the Jews of Iraq from the homeland of which they had been a part for over three millennia in the space of some twelve months between the summer of 1950 and the summer of 1951. The story gains added poignancy from being told by another victim of Zionism, a Palestinian Muslim from Haifa. Although the connection may not be immediately obvious, the fact is that both events, the expulsion of the Jews from Iraq, and the expulsion of the Palestinians from Palestine, are two sides of the same coin, in that neither sets of events of actions would have taken place but for the desire on the part of the Zionists to have a land of their own, which would be populated by the Jews of the world, who would have the chance to create a new and vibrant society where they could express their Jewish identity socially, culturally, and religiously, and above all without fear of persecution.

Without, one can be fairly sure, even remotely anticipating the consequences of the commitment it was making, the British government had stated on 2 November 1917 that it would 'view with favour the establishment in Palestine of a national home for the Jewish people … it being clearly understood that nothing should be done which prejudice the civil and religious rights of existing non-Jewish communities in Palestine …' As we know, this dual commitment, reproduced word for word in the mandate for Palestine (14 July 1922), proved impossible to fulfil, since to do so necessarily and actually involved a zero-sum game (a phrase not then in vogue but apposite nevertheless) in which any concessions to the demands of the Palestinians directly damaged the interests of the Zionists, and *vice versa*. Each community believed that Britain's primary duty was to advance that particular community's interests, and matters gradually deteriorated through the mandate, with communal hostilities gradually worsening, interrupted only temporarily by the Second World War.

In the course of the war, American Jewry identified itself closely and definitively with Zionism, especially after news of the extent of the horror of the Holocaust began to spread to the rest of the world at the end of 1942. Although the United States would not change its immigration laws to accept Jewish refugees, President Truman took up the cause of the survivors of the concentration camps, urging that they should be admitted to Palestine. The British government were opposed to this, fearing a recurrence of the armed Arab opposition of the late 1930s. In addition, immigration on such a scale was contrary to British policy, which was generally to support some version of the partition plan first floated by the Peel Commission in 1937. By the mid-1940s, it had become increasingly clear to the younger Zionist leaders that they would have to use force in order to persuade the British to evacuate Palestine. It was also becoming clear, as Albert Hourani remarked to the Anglo-American Commission late in 1945, that 'no room can be made in Palestine for a second nation except by dislodging or exterminating the first.' By February 1947, partly because of the immobility caused by the widening policy gap between Britain and the United States, Britain handed the problem over to the United Nations. Some six months later the United Nations called for the end of the mandate and the adoption of a partition plan somewhat more generous to the Zionists than the British had devised in 1937. In September 1947 Britain declared its intention to withdraw from Palestine, and the United Nations voted for partition (rather than a single bi-national state) at the end of November. The British withdrew on 14 May 1948, and the state of Israel was proclaimed the next day. By that time, some 300,000 Palestinian Arabs had fled, and a further 430,000 would leave by the end of the year. Slightly over half went into 'temporary' camps in the Gaza strip and what became known as the West Bank, while the rest took refuge on the East Bank of the Jordan or in the neighbouring Arab states.[1] By 1952, tensions in the

---

1. See Charles D. Smith, *Palestine and the Arab-Israeli Conflict: a History with Documents*, 5th edition, Boston and New York, Bedford/St Martin's, 2004, pp. 20–216, for a readable and comprehensive account of these events.

region had made life increasingly intolerable in their own countries for the Jews of the Middle East; some 325,000 Jews from the Arab world had taken refuge in Israel, about 125,000 of whom came from Iraq.

Recent works such as Mark Cohen's *Under Crescent and Cross* ...[1] have painted a more realistic picture of the state of Jewish-Muslim relations, and the conditions of Jewish life, during the Middle Ages than earlier and more starry-eyed propagandists would have had us believe. At the very least, however, the Jews in the Muslim world had a more stable and less uncertain existence than their co-religionists in medieval and early modern Europe. In eighteenth century Aleppo, Abraham Marcus tells us,

> The religious differences, stressed and exaggerated in so many ways, did not separate the communities into segregated social worlds of their own. Their divisive effects were limited by the great similarities between Aleppines of different religious persuasions, and by the pragmatism that guided daily behavior. The confessional boundaries were so clearly drawn and religious beliefs so little open to debate that people could associate freely in various spheres without compromise. Sharing a common cultural heritage, Muslims, Christians and Jews were hardly strangers to each other. Their religions, based as they were on many of the same traditions, instilled in them similar moral visions and social ideals.[2]

In eighteenth and nineteenth century Aleppo and Damascus, Muslims and Jews were often business partners, as well as members of the same occupational guilds.[3] In addition, as emerges from the

---

1. Mark R. Cohen, *Under Crescent and Cross: the Jews in the Middle Ages*, Princeton NJ, Princeton University Press, 1994.
2. Abraham Marcus, *The Middle East on the Eve of Modernity: Aleppo in the Eighteenth Century*, New York, Columbia University Press, 1989, p. 43.
3. See Abdul-Karim Rafeq, 'Craft organisation, work ethics and the strains of change in Ottoman Syria,' *Journal of the American Oriental Society*, 111 (1991),
(continued...)

quarter by quarter description of Aleppo around 1900 by the historian Kamil al-Ghazzi,[1] while some of the quarters (especially those next to the synagogue or close to the various churches) were mostly Jewish or mostly Christian, none were *entirely* Jewish or Christian, showing that what segregation existed was voluntary rather than compulsory. Even more pertinently, similar patterns of partnership and co-residence are visible in late nineteenth-century Haifa, which had already become an important destination for Zionist immigration.[2]

When it emerged in its modern form at the end of the nineteenth century, Zionism had very little appeal to the Jews of the Middle East.[3] It is fair to say that Abraham Marcus's view (in the long quotation above) of the common *Weltanschauung* of Middle Eastern townspeople regardless of sectarian affiliation generally holds good until the Palestine revolt of 1936–39. At that point (which coincided with the wider diffusion of wireless broadcasting) the conflict began to impinge more generally on the collective consciousness of the region, and its broader implications for Middle Eastern Jewry began to be more widely perceived, both by Jews and non-Jews. It is significant that one of the major vehicles of 'modernity' for the Jewish communities of the Middle East, the Alliance Israélite Universelle, which founded schools from Casablanca to Teheran,

---

(...continued)
    pp. 495–511.

1. Kamil al-Ghazzi, *Nahr al-Dhahab fi Tarikh Halab*, Aleppo, 1926. The figures have been tabulated in Heinz Gaube and Eugen Wirth, *Aleppo: Historische und geographische Beiträge zur baulichen Gestaltung, zur sozialen Organisation und zur wirtschaftlichen Dynamik einer vorderasiatischen Fernhandelsmetropole*, Wiesbaden, Dr Ludwig Reichert Verlag, 1984, pp. 427–41. Similar (if less detailed) evidence emerges from other Ottoman cities.

2. Mahmoud Yazbak, *Haifa in the late Ottoman period, 1864–1914: a Muslim town in transition*, Leiden, Brill, 1998.

3. There were some exceptions, particularly among the Jewish communities of Morocco and Yemen, some of whose members were attracted to a mystical form of Zionism – although this was an ideology far removed from that of Pinsker or Herzl. For aspects of early Yemeni immigration, see Gershon Shafir, *Land, Labor and the Origins of the Israeli-Palestinian Conflict 1882–1914*, Berkeley and Los Angeles, University of California Press, 1996, pp. 91–122.

was decidedly 'assimilationist', and regarded Zionism as a tiresome distraction; its mission was to educate Jews in European, particularly French, culture, and it had little or no interest in its students' souls.[1]

To return for a moment to the group whom I described meeting at the beginning of this essay: I mentioned that they had all been associated with the Iraqi Communist Party. From this it is reasonable to extrapolate that the members of the group felt as Iraqi as any other Iraqi, and felt fully entitled to participate in the politics of the country where they (and of course their ancestors for thousands of years) had lived. Although historians are not supposed to speculate about what might have happened, I think I can reasonably assume that had the state of Israel come into being in a less ambitious fashion (as part of a bi-national Arab-Jewish state, for example), it would never have occurred to more than a handful of Iraqi Jews to leave Iraq. While it makes little sense to blame the Balfour Declaration for all the disasters which have occurred since 1917, it is worth remembering that the phrase 'it being clearly understood that nothing shall be done which may prejudice the civil and religious rights of existing non-Jewish communities in Palestine' is followed by 'or the rights and political status of Jews in any other country.'[2]

One of the most famous slogans of early Zionism, coined by the 'Anglo-Jewish writer' Israel Zangwill, was that Palestine was 'a land without a people for a people without a land'. It was often alleged by

---

1. See Aron Rodrigue, *French Jews, Turkish Jews: the Alliance Israélite Universelle and the politics of Jewish schooling in Turkey, 1860–1925*, Bloomington, IN, Indiana University Press, 1990.
2. For Edwin Montagu, Secretary of State for India, the only Jew in Lloyd George's Cabinet in 1917, 'the Declaration [was] an intolerable threat to his peace of mind'; he regarded it as forcing him back to the ghetto. He wrote to Lloyd George on October 4, a month before the Declaration was published: '... If you make a statement about Palestine as the National Home for the Jews, every anti-Semitic organisation and newspaper will ask what right a Jewish Englishman, with the status at best of a naturalized foreigner, has to take a foremost part in the government of the British Empire ...' Leonard Stein, *The Balfour Declaration*, London, Vallentine, Mitchell, 1961, pp. 497–98, 500.

those who should have known better that one of the reasons which led Britain to favour Zionism and Balfour himself to issue the Declaration on 2 November 1917 was some sort of naïve belief on the part of a patrician politician thousands of miles away that Palestine was sparsely inhabited and that there was thus 'plenty of room' for immigration. In fact, in the middle of a long Memorandum on the future of Syria, Palestine and Mesopotamia dated 11 August 1919, Balfour wrote:

> The four Great Powers are committed to Zionism. And Zionism, be it right or wrong, good or bad, is rooted in age-long traditions, in present needs, in future hopes, of far profounder import than the desires and prejudices of the 700,000 Arabs who now inhabit that ancient land. In my opinion, that is right.[1]

Zangwill, who had visited Palestine, could still write in 1920:

> … [in Palestine] there is no Arab people living in intimate fusion with the country, utilising its resources and stamping it with a characteristic impress: there is at best an Arab encampment.

In *Expulsion of the Palestinians*, from which the quotation from Zangwill is taken, Nur Masalha considers that such statements were not intended to be taken literally: '[Those who made them] did not mean that there were no people in Palestine, but that there were no people worth considering within the framework of the notions of European supremacy that then held sway.'[2] In addition, the Zionists could hardly have been unaware of the opposition which their activities had aroused among the Palestinian Arabs almost from the

---

1. *Documents on British Foreign Policy, 1918–1939,* 1st series, London, H.M. Stationery Office, Vol. IV, 1952, no 242, pp. 340–49.
2. Nur Masalha, *Expulsion of the Palestinians; the Concept of 'Transfer' in Zionist Thought, 1882–1948*, Washington DC, Institute of Palestine Studies, 1992, p. 6.

beginning of the first *Aliyah*. In a speech after the end of the First World in 1918, David Ben-Gurion remarked ominously that 'there is no solution to the question of relations between Arabs and Jews … We as a nation want this country to be ours; the Arabs, as a nation, want this country to be theirs.'[1]

Over the next few decades, the implications of such statements were taken a stage further, and 'solutions' involving population transfer were embraced first by politicians on the outer edges of the political spectrum but then fairly rapidly by mainstream technocrats and political figures.[2] Masalha shows that the Zionist Executive began its first detailed consideration of population transfer in the wake of the report of the Peel Commission recommending partition, published in July 1937. In November that year, the Executive set up a Transfer Committee, among whose members was Yosef Weitz, director of the Land Department of the Jewish National Fund, the body most closely concerned with purchasing Arab land.[3] At a meeting on 21 November 1937, Weitz advocated 'transferring' the indigenous agricultural population to the 'Arab state' (that is, as envisaged in the Peel Commission's partition scheme) and/or to Transjordan, Syria, and Iraq, in order to open up land for Zionist settlement. This was not to be carried out by force (although some of Weitz's fellow-committee members were rather less squeamish) but by joint agreements with the neighbouring states, with the sweetener of various economic inducements. Alfred Bonné, a prominent economist charged with investigating the financial and procedural aspects of this operation, declared that 'all the Arabs must be removed within ten years'. Such discussions lost urgency with the British government's abandonment of the partition solution

---

1. Neil Caplan, *Palestine Jewry and the Arab Question 1918–1925*, London, 1925, p. 42, quoted in Charles D. Smith, *Palestine and the Arab-Israeli Conflict*, p. 117
2. Including the economists Alfred Bonné, Avram Granovsky/Granott and Arthur Ruppin, and prominent political figures like David Ben-Gurion, Berl Katznelson, Moshe Shertok, and Menahim Ussishkin.
3. The Department's land-purchasing activities have been studied in detail by Kenneth W. Stein; see *The Land Question in Palestine, 1917–1939*, Chapel Hill, University of North Carolina Press, 1984, especially pp. 173–211.

late in 1938, and also with the White Paper of 1939, which 'represents Britain's retreat from its position of total support for the Jewish national home.'[1]

A prominent principle of the early years of the Zionist movement was that of the 'conquest of labour', the idea that Jewish labour would create a new society for the future Jewish nation. The idea of employing Jewish labour in Jewish agricultural or industrial enterprises was a key tenet of the trade union organisation, the *Histadrut*, founded by the merger of two existing institutions in 1920. However, before the First World War, some of the larger Jewish agricultural enterprises had tried to solve some of the problems caused by the higher cost, the scarcity, and/or the incompetence, of Ashkenazi immigrants from Eastern Europe, many of whom had found the conditions too hard and had returned to their homes. Agudat Netaim (The Planters' Society), the largest capitalist enterprise during the Second *Aliya*, according to Gershon Shafir, attempted to import Yemeni Jewish workers to work on its plantations. Yemenis could speak both Arabic and Hebrew; they were Ottoman citizens; they were used to agricultural work, and, perhaps the clincher, they would be 'content with little'; they could be paid Arab rates while simultaneously enabling their employers to dismiss the Arab labourers.[2] However, as Shafir shows, they were so very poorly paid that it was difficult for them to feed their families, and no housing had been constructed for them; in addition, they frequently displaced more expensive Ashkenazi workers, who required some 50 per cent more wages. The implication here is that even before the British mandate there was a clear pecking order among Jews, with the Yemeni or Middle Eastern Jews considered second-class citizens.

Although the idea of 'transfer' dropped out of sight in the late 1930s, it had certainly not been abandoned, particularly not by Yosef Weitz of the JNF, whose diaries (now in the Central Zionist Archive) and correspondence now seem almost prophetic:

---

1. Masalha, *Expulsion of the Palestinians*, pp. 93–119, 125.
2. Shafir, *Land, Labor*, pp. 99–106.

Amongst ourselves it must be clear that there is no room for both peoples in this country ... The only way is to transfer the Arabs from here to neighbouring countries ... And the transfer must be done through their absorption in Iraq and Syria and even in Transjordan. (20 December 1940)[1]

The JNF's own programme of regular purchases of land in Palestine, he noted in February 1941, would not be sufficient to solve the problem. Weitz mentions Iraq, the Syrian Jazira (where large scale settlement of Bedouin and Kurdish tribes had begun in the 1930s under the auspices of the French mandate) and Transjordan[2] as possible destinations. Of particular interest in the context of Abbas Shiblak's book are the detailed plans for settling Palestinian Arabs in Iraq, set out by the American Jewish millionaire Edward Norman, put forward as early as 1934 and elaborated further in the late 1930s and 1940s. As we know, these came to nothing; writing in February 1941 James Sterndale Bennett of the Colonial Office thought the plan hopelessly impractical; 'there was not the slightest reason to assume that the Palestinian Arabs would accept a voluntary transfer, or that the Iraqi government, with its known pan-Arab sentiments, would ask for their evacuation to Iraq.'[3] In spite of its evident absurdity to anyone familiar with the situation on the ground, the plan to settle Palestinians in Iraq gained the support of former president Herbert Hoover, was submitted to the White House in November 1945, and, as we shall see, even briefly considered by Britain in 1949–50.

---

1. Unless referenced otherwise, quotations from Weitz's diary and references to the transfer plans of Edward Norman and others in the 1940s are based on material in Masalha, *Expulsion of the Palestinians*, pp. 125ff.
2. In spite of regular denials in the Arab press that such transactions had taken place, Amir 'Abdullah of Transjordan had been receiving regular backhanders from the Jewish Agency since 1933 in the form of payments from the (Zionist) Palestine Land Development Company for options on land in the Ghawr al-Kibd on the east bank of the Jordan. See Avi Shlaim, *The Politics of Partition: King Abdullah, the Zionists and Palestine 1921–1951*, Oxford, Oxford University Press, 1990, pp. 48–51.
3. Masalha, *Expulsion of the Palestinians*, p. 154.

One of the main contributions of recent research on the events of 1948 has been to show that, far from being some sort of convenient miracle, the 'departure', to put it as neutrally as possible, of most of the Arab population of Palestine in 1948, had long been in the forefront of the minds of many of the most influential of those who steered Israel to independence in 1948. The recent historiography of the Palestinian exodus, both in the tentative conclusions of Benny Morris and the more trenchant assessments of Nur Masalha[1] agrees that local actions by Haganah commanders, and in some cases the deliberate and direct orders of the Zionist leadership, played an important part in Palestinian flight. Morris acknowledges that there is no truth in the allegation that the Palestinian leadership urged the Palestinians to leave their homes, but he has also found 'no blanket orders handed down from above for the systematic expulsion of the Palestinians'. Masalha goes further, but he is only able to hint at the existence of a more comprehensive plan.[2]

Between April 1939 and the end of December 1945, of the total of 54,700 Jews entering Palestine, about 12,500 were from the Middle East and North Africa (4,200 from Turkey, 4,500 from Yemen, 1,595 from Iraq, and 620 from Iran).[3] Between 1919 and 14 May 1948, 450,000 Jews had immigrated to Israel, some 380,000 from Europe and 45,000 from the whole of Asia and Africa. Given the wide chronological spread it is difficult to assess how many of the Europeans were holocaust survivors; Jewish Agency figures

---

1. Benny Morris, *The Birth of the Palestinian Refugee Problem 1947–1949*, Cambridge, Cambridge University Press, 1989; Masalha, *Expulsion of the Palestinians*, especially Chapter 5, 'The 1948 Exodus', pp. 174–205.
2. Avi Shlaim, 'The debate about 1948' in Ilan Pappé (ed.), *The Israel Palestine Question*, London, Routledge, 1999, pp. 171–92; see also Nur Masalha, 'A critique on Benny Morris', pp. 211–20 in the same collection.
3. Justin McCarthy, *The Population of Palestine: Population Statistics of the Late Ottoman Period and the Mandate,* New York, Columbia University Press, 1990, Table A9-5, p. 174. It is not clear whether these figures include illegal immigrants.

show some 250,000 immigrants arriving between 1932 and 1946.[1] In the six months between 15 May and 31 December 1948, 77,000 arrived from Europe and 13,000 from Asia and Africa. Between 1949 and 1958, a further 326,000 arrived from Europe, the overwhelming majority between 1949 and 1951.[2] 268,000 came from Asia and Africa; again, the overwhelming majority arrived between 1949–51. In the last large migration until the arrival of the Soviet Jews in the 1990s, 69,000 Jews from 'Africa' came in 1956 and 1957, presumably mostly from Egypt, Libya and the Maghrib, at least partly as a consequence of Suez.[3] The migration of Jews from the Arab world accounted for some 45 per cent of all immigrants in the three years 1949, 1950, and 1951; of these, almost half, some 125,000, came from Iraq in 1950 and 1951.

In brief, life became increasingly intolerable for Iraqi Jews after 1948. Of course, as Shiblak shows, the creation of Israel was in many ways a godsend to the Iraqi governments of the day. It was enormously convenient, in the late 1940s and early 1950s, for them to deflect popular hostility at their corruption and incompetence by constant invocations of the threat posed by the Zionist enemy, and, in time, by the potential Zionist fifth column within the country. Right-wing pan-Arab nationalism, one of the least attractive survivors of the Second World War, was marshalled to rail against 'Communists, Zionists and Jews'.[4] For a while, Iraqi Jews hoped that a peace settlement in Palestine would allow things to return to normal, but it soon became clear that this was not going to happen. As with their co-religionists elsewhere, the Iraqi Jews became the objects of a widespread Zionist campaign intended to convince

1. McCarthy, *Population of Palestine*, Table 2.13 p. 34.
2. I do not have access to a breakdown of their countries of origin, but it can be assumed that most were from the newly created people's democracies in Eastern Europe, particularly Poland and Rumania.
3. See V.D. Segre, *Israel; a Society in Transition*, London, Oxford University Press, 1971, p. 215. The figures are taken from the Statistical Abstract of Israel (Jerusalem, 1961).
4. Given the strength of the Iraqi Communist Party (and the onset of the Cold War), Communism was evidently regarded as the more serious threat, although Zionist affiliation was made a criminal offence in July 1948.

doubters that their only safety lay in emigrating to Israel, that they would always be vulnerable if they stayed where they were. Shiblak also shows that the bomb attacks in Baghdad against Jewish lives and properties in 1951 were organised by Zionist activists, sent from Israel with the sanction of senior Israeli politicians. In addition, there is ample evidence that both Britain and the USA pressed the Iraqi government to 'facilitate' Jewish emigration. Britain made no protest against the Denaturalisation Law of 1950, and for some months beforehand the Foreign Office had been toying with fanciful schemes of 'population exchange' whose palpable absurdity took an astonishingly long time to come to the surface. By March 1951, again without British protest – and even with a measure of British connivance – the government of Iraq froze the assets of Jews who had applied to give up their Iraqi nationality (that is, who had applied to leave Iraq). Given the intransigent attitude of the Israelis towards the Palestinians and the property which they had been forced to leave behind, neither Britain nor the United States felt it useful to protest against similar actions on the part of the government of Iraq.

Like the Yemenis before them, most members of the first generation of Iraqi Jewish immigrants, of whom over 50 per cent were literate compared with the 15 per cent literacy among all Iraqis, did not find life easy in Israel. Constantly made aware of their inferior status, they were generally assigned to the new settlement townships, and were often obliged to put up with living standards considerably lower than they had been accustomed to at home. Their resentment was shared by many of their fellow non-Ashkenazis, and the 'revolt of the Oriental Jews' eventually became a major factor in the election of Menachim Begin's conservative Likud government in 1977; until then, Israel had been governed by a series of coalitions whose orientations were generally 'social democratic'.

It is a shabby, squalid and deeply tragic story, of betrayal, manipulation and doctrinaire opportunism, mirrored almost perfectly by the fate of the Palestinians. It is much to Abbas Shiblak's credit, and a measure of his own humanity, that he has managed to capture the essence of the fate of the Iraqi Jews with such profound sympathy. As with many other Palestinians, his journey has been in so many ways a mirror image of their own.

November 2004

Introduction

Before 1948 there were about eight hundred thousand Jews (roughly 6 per cent of the world's total) living in Arab countries. They did not constitute a single ethnic group, however, for they differed in origin, came to live in the Arab countries at different periods of history, and occupied varying positions in the societies in which they lived.

The roots of the indigenous groups among them (Yemeni and Iraqi Jews, for instance) can be traced back centuries before Christ. In the fifteenth century after Christ, following the collapse of Arab rule in Spain, waves of Sephardic Jews emigrated, mainly to Arab North Africa and Egypt, where they were soon assimilated into the new environment. Finally, groups of European Ashkenazi Jews settled in the Arab world during the nineteenth and early twentieth centuries as part of the colonial presence. The cultural and social characteristics of these groups approximated those of the foreign European communities, and the bulk of these European Jewish communities went back to their countries of origin when the colonial presence ended.

By contrast, the cultural affinities of Jews and Muslims, as well as their similar socio-economic background, facilitated the integration of the indigenous Jewish communities, which were Arabized in many respects. The term 'Arab Jew' is therefore probably appropriate, and in the areas of Ottoman rule, they had the right to administer their communal affairs under the *millah* system.

Arab Jews played an important role during the period of the Abbasid caliphate and through most of the centuries of Ottoman rule. They worked in commerce, crafts, and credit and money exchanges, while the enlightened middle strata secured a significant share of public office. Because of their occupational structure, most Jews tended to be concentrated in towns and cities, but many others lived in rural areas as farmers, especially in Kurdistan, Yemen, and the interior of North Africa.

For many years Zionism, which emerged from historical conditions peculiar to Europe, had little impact on Jews in Arab countries. Later, however, the establishment of a Jewish state in Palestine proved to have more dramatic and far-reaching consequences for these Jewish communities than for any others. From 1948 onwards, Arab Jews left their countries in successive waves, going mainly to Israel. The two most deeply-rooted communities – in Yemen and Iraq – were evacuated *en masse* between 1949 and 1951.

Official Israeli estimates (see the 1961 census) put the number of oriental Jews living in Palestine in 1948 at 44,809, or 10.4 per cent of the total Jewish population of 452,158. But their relative numbers have increased rapidly since then, and oriental Jews now constitute more than 60 per cent of Israel's Jewish population. Meanwhile, estimates of the number of Jews still living in Arab countries vary widely. The American Jewish Yearbook (AJY) made estimates in 1968 and 1971. These are given in columns 1 and 2 of the table below. The third column gives the estimates of the periodical *al-Ard* in 1975 (vol. 3, no. 1, 21 September 1975, p. 113). My own estimate, given in column 4, is a reconciliation of these figures based on a number of recent reports in periodicals and newspaper accounts.

Jewish Population in Arab Countries

Country	1	2	3	4
Algeria	2000	1000	1000	1500
Egypt	2000	1900	500	2000
Iraq	6000	2500	500	300
Lebanon	7000	2000	1800	2500
Morocco	55000	–	31000	40000
Sudan	–	–	–	1000
Syria	4000	4000	4000	4000
Tunisia	20000	10000	8000	9000
Yemen	1000	500	–	3000
Total	97000	21900	46800	63300

The Jewish exodus from Arab countries cannot be understood in terms of the models typically used to analyse mass migrations. It was not caused, for instance, by shifts of borders, as happened in Europe between the two world wars. Nor can it be likened to the European settlement in America, Australia, or Africa in the eighteenth and nineteenth centuries, fundamentally an outflow of rural population stimulated by rising population pressures on limited means of subsistence. There are some similarities between European overseas settlement and Jewish settlement in Palestine before the thirties, but the analogy collapses in the case of the emigration of Arab Jews. Especially in the more established communities like that of Iraq, few Jews saw Palestine as more economically rewarding than their own countries, in which they enjoyed prominent positions in social and economic life.

The closest analogy to the emigration of Arab Jews is the transfer of population caused by the drawing of new borders based on racial or religious distinctions, as in the Indian subcontinent, whose partition was followed by the two-way traffic of Hindus and Muslims.

The mass emigration of Arab Jews can be understood only in the light of the establishment of Israel and the armed and political hostilities that followed. But this is itself one of the difficulties in examining this emigration, since the various explanations for the exodus are themselves intertwined with the political confrontation that arose as a result of the conflict in Palestine.

Pro-Zionist sources, for instance, see the emigration of Arab Jews as the result of a long history of oppression and racial and religious prejudice. Zionist activists among the Arab Jewish communities tend to stress the importance of ideological commitment to Zionism as a motivation for the exodus. Both versions frequently rewrite history in the aftermath of the Arab-Israeli conflict.

On the other hand, the emigration of Arab Jews has not received adequate attention from Arab scholars. With very few exceptions, Arab authors consider the emigration the result of Zionist activities and propaganda. Significantly, they have generally failed to take account of the position taken within the Arab national movement and to evaluate Arab government policies critically. Most arguments of this type display a lack of understanding of Zionism and consequently underestimate the extent to which the policies of Arab governments were self-defeating.

Rather than dealing with the emigration of Arab Jewish communities in general, this book focuses on one of the most deep-rooted of these communities, examining the circumstances that led to its mass exodus between the summer of 1950 and the summer of 1951.

The Jewish presence in Iraq goes back more than 2,500 years. In fact, there was a time when Jewish scholarship in Iraq was the ultimate spiritual authority for world Jewry. The renowned Babylonian Talmud was produced there, as were some of the most outstanding Jewish literary works. Learned rabbis presided over the great Jewish academies of Sura and Pumbedita, and the exilarchs too resided in those centres. Jewish history refers to the first five centuries of Islam as the 'Gaonic period', because the heads of the two academies were known as Gaons, considered by Jews throughout the world as the ultimate authorities on all matters pertaining to religion, which then included civil law as well. The Iraqi Jews continuously maintained their communal identity and were among the wealthiest and most fully integrated of all Jewish communities in Arab countries. They played a major cultural, social, and economic role in the life of Mesopotamia and of modern Iraq alike.

Because of these and other factors, the Jewish exodus from Iraq, more than any other, offers a rich opportunity to understand the circumstances of Arab Jewish emigration to Israel. Iraq's proximity to the conflict in Palestine, its direct involvement in the 1948 war, and the connection made at one stage between the destiny of Iraqi Jews and proposals to settle the Palestinian question link events in Iraq closely to those in Palestine. Moreover, Iraq in the late forties and early fifties was a showcase of the crisis of the Arab ruling class at the time, still under colonial influence and riddled by various competing factions of the Arab national movement. Finally, the dramatic nature of the exit of the Jewish community distinguishes it from other cases.

The Iraqi situation also illustrates the complexity of factors involved: the impact of the colonial legacy and the advance of Zionism on the position of the Jews; the attitudes of the different factions of the Arab national movement, as well as the policies of the Arab governments. More important, it illustrates the way these factors interacted and affected the Jewish community during the crucial years just prior to the exodus.

In writing this book, I have had access to a wide variety of sources.

Extensive use has been made of British Foreign Office (FO) documents recently made available in the Public Record Office (PRO). These shed light on some of the more obscure aspects of the subject, especially events following the establishment of Israel and leading to the exodus.

Relevant official documents and newspaper sources available in the Iraqi National Archives have also been examined. These provide additional insight, particularly into the political involvement of the Jewish intelligentsia in the late 1940s, and into the attitudes of the nationalists and the Iraqi press to the Jews.

Unpublished manuscripts also helped to fill some of the gaps. Interviews and discussions with Iraqi Jews now living in England were of great help.

ONE

The Jews of Iraq

The boundaries of modern Iraq, formerly known as Mesopotamia, were drawn as part of the territorial division effected by the victorious colonial powers after the first world war. Home of some of the world's oldest civilizations, it has been subjected to numerous foreign conquests and has hosted many immigrant groups. As a result, Iraq contains more ethnic and religious groups than any other Arab country.

The Jews of Iraq formed a homogeneous community and were able to maintain their communal identity, their culture, and their traditions through the centuries. There was little conversion to other religions.[1] No immigrants settled in Iraq when the Sephardic wave of immigration spread through most provinces of the Ottoman empire during the fifteenth century, nor did Iraq witness the arrival of large numbers of European Jews during the colonial era. This is in sharp contrast to Egypt and other countries of Arab North Africa, where Sephardic and European immigrants mixed with and, to varying degrees, affected the character of the indigenous Jewish communities. In Egypt, for example, the number of foreign Jewish

---

1. Some 'Islamicization' had occurred in earlier centuries, and during the 1930s and 1940s some Jews embraced the Bahai creed. These, however, were rare cases and do not compare with the forced renunciation of the Jewish faith which has taken place during the last hundred years among Persian Jews, or during the Enlightenment in Europe (see Cohen, 1966b, p. 207).

nationals in 1917 was estimated at 34,601 (58.1 per cent of the total Jewish population of 59,507); 12 per cent of the French who arrived in Algeria after its occupation in 1830 were Jews (Cohen, 1973, p. 48). The number and influence of European Jews in both countries rose steadily thereafter.

Among the Jewish communities in Arab countries, the Yemeni Jews were probably the only ones as deeply rooted and uniform in origin as the Iraqis. But the Yemenis lacked the wealth, extent of culture and integration, and openness toward the world that Iraqis enjoyed.

Although they preserved their communal identity, the Iraqi Jews were well-integrated and indigenous to the country. Socially and culturally, they formed an inseparable part of its history, and they left their imprint on various aspects of Iraqi life. They were thoroughly Arabized in the sense that their tradition, superstitions, and language were Arabic. Their dialect, which is close to that of Mosul district, is considered by some to be among the purest, closest to that of the Arabian peninsula. They also used Arabic in their hymns and religious ceremonies.

Demographic Changes

It is difficult to ascertain the precise number of Jews in Iraq. In 1920 the British administration estimated Iraq's total population at 1,754,500, with the Jewish population said to be 58,000.[1] But these figures were advanced immediately after the British occupation and could hardly have covered all the distant areas where many Iraqis (Jews among them) then lived in an effort to avoid the Ottoman capitation tax. Other estimates (Ghanima, 1924, p. 183) estimated a Jewish community of 87,488 for the same period.

Official Iraqi statistics, based on the 1947 census, said that the Jewish community numbered 118,000, or 2.6 per cent of the total

---

1. India Office, extracted from 'Note on Mobilization in Mesopotamia, 1918–1920', dated 13 June 1920, Appendix A, FO 371/5076, E 8136/13/46.

population of 4.5 million (see Table 1). There are those, however, who believe that the 1947 census was not completely accurate and was not always properly conducted. Some unofficial sources suggest that it is likely that the real number of Jews in the late forties was ten to twenty thousand higher than the official figure.[1]

Until the beginning of the twentieth century, the Jews of Iraq lived in their own quarters in the main cities, but these quarters bore no resemblance to the Jewish ghettos of Europe. Rather, as H. Batatu put it (Batatu, 2004, pp. 17–19), urban life in Iraq was dominated by the *mahallah*, or city quarter, which reflected communal cleavages. Different sects, classes, and tribal or ethnic groups tended to live in their own separate *mahallahs*.[2] The social and economic life of each of these groups tended to revolve around the *mahallah*.

But economic and educational developments gradually eroded the *mahallah*. At the turn of the century, Jews began to move out to Muslim and Christian quarters and vice versa. This process gathered speed after the first world war. An envoy of the Jewish Agency who visited Baghdad from time to time to collect funds noted in 1946: 'Baghdad looked different, it has grown and the Jews are spread in various districts, specially in modern surroundings' (quoted by Twena, 1975, p. 170).

---

1. See a report written by Shaul Sasson, the son of the chief rabbi, dated 14 December 1950, in which he estimated the number of the Iraqi Jews at about 150,000. FO 371/82431, EQ 147/58.

2. For example, the Shi'is lived in al-Dahanah, Sababig-al-Al, al-Queshed, Suq-al-Attarin and other quarters on Baghdad's eastern bank. The Jews lived mostly in al-Tawat, Taht-al-Takyah, Abu Saifain and Suq Hannun, and the Christians in Agd-al-Nasarah and Ras-al-Qaryah. The Sunnis, who lived in the rest of the eastern side of the city, were subdivided along different lines. The Turkish military resided in al-Maydan, the aristocratic families and upper officials in Dukkan Shnawah, artisans in inner Bab-al-Shaikh, and Baghdadi army officers of humble origins and other elements in Bab-al-Shaikh's outer fringes. The division was even narrower among the artisans, who were organized loosely in *asnaf*, or guilds, members of the same craft, like members of the same family, tending to reside in the same street.

Table 1: Religious and Ethnic Composition of Iraq in 1947 (in 000s)

Denomination	Urban	%	Rural	%	Total	%
Muslims						
Arab Shi'i	673	41.9	1761	56.5	2434	51.4
Arab Sunni	428	26.7	472	16	900	19.7
Kurd Sunni	176	10.9	664	22.4	840	18.4
Persian Shi'i	49	3.1	3	0.1	52	1.2
Turkoman Sunni	39	2.5	11	0.3	50	1.1
Turkoman Shi'i	11	0.7	31	1.1	42	0.9
Fayli Kurd Shi'i	14	0.9	16	0.5	30	0.6
Non-Muslims						
Christians	94	5.9	55	1.8	149	3.1
Jews	114	7	4	0.2	118	2.6
Yazidis and Shabaks	2	0.1	31	1	33	0.8
Sabeans	5	0.3	2	0.1	7	0.2
Total	1605	100	2960	100	4655	100

Source: Batatu (2004, p. 40), based on Ministry of Social Affairs, 1947 census, Baghdad, 1954.

Two main demographic changes had occurred since the mid-nineteenth century. First, there was considerable internal emigration from north to south following the opening of the Suez Canal, which shifted commercial pathways from the overland route (from Europe to India via Aleppo in Syria and Mosul in northern Iraq) to the naval route, thus favouring the Iraqi port of Basra. North-to-south emigration was also encouraged by changes introduced during the reign of the Ottoman *wali* (governor) Midhat Pasha (1869–72). These included land reforms, the establishment of modern schools, the pacification of tribes in central and southern Iraq, and the protection of cities from Bedouin attack.

Second, rapid urbanization occurred after the first world war. Waves of migration from rural areas led to a substantial increase in the population of Baghdad, Basra, and (to a lesser extent) Mosul.

As economic conditions in the north began to deteriorate at the end of the nineteenth century, Jews, like others, started to move south. In the middle of the nineteenth century, there had been only two small Jewish communities in all of southern Iraq (in Basra and in Hilla), but by the turn of the century these two communities had grown larger and additional communities settled in Amara, Qalat Salih, Ali al-Gharbi, and Musayyab.

For the first time, Jews began to settle in Shi'ite religious centres such as Najaf (Mu'allim, 1980). Except for Basra, however, the Jewish movement south ebbed after the first world war. According to the 1947 census, there were only 5,473 Jews in four of the southern districts (Amara 2,131; Muntafik 652; Hilla 1,865; Diwaniyah 825).

The largest Jewish community in Iraq was in the capital city of Baghdad.[1] In 1848 the traveller Benjamin Ben Joseph put the number of Jewish families there at three thousand. The British estimated that there were fifty thousand Jews in Baghdad in 1920, and according to the 1947 census there were then 77,542. There is no doubt that the number of Jews in Baghdad rose steadily. Apart from the factors already mentioned, this persistent growth was accelerated by some migration of Jews from Iran (during the second half of the nineteenth century) and from the Kurdish region and southern districts of Iraq itself after the first world war.

There were 4,670 Jews in the remaining central districts in 1920, and 4,681 according to the 1947 census (Diyalah 2,851; Dulaym 1,442; Kut 349; Karbala 39).

Scores of small Jewish communities were scattered through northern Iraq, the largest in the city of Mosul (with 450 families in 1848 according to Benjamin Ben Joseph). The population remained stable at approximately three thousand until the beginning of the twentieth century. The decline of the economic standing of Mosul seems to have contributed to the departure of Jews for Baghdad and, in a few cases, for Europe.

---

1. Unless otherwise attributed, the source for the estimates given in the remainder of this section is Ben-Ya'acov, 1965.

After the development of the oil industry in the north following the first world war, there was some migration of Jews to smaller towns in the northern region. According to official figures, there were 13,833 Jews in all the northern districts in 1920, and 19,767 according to the 1947 census (including Arbil 3,109; Sulaymaniah 2,271; Kirkuk 4,042).

In 1920 about 66 per cent of the Jews of Iraq lived in the cities of Baghdad and Basra. About 74 per cent resided in those two cities and 22.5 per cent in other cities, according to the 1947 census. The remaining 3.5 per cent lived in areas defined by the Iraqi authorities as rural.

Most of the rural dwellers were Kurdish Jews who lived mainly in two northern districts – Mosul and Kirkuk – 20.1 per cent of whose Jewish population resided in rural areas.[1] This contrasts with only 1.2 per cent of Jews in rural areas in southern and central districts.

Although Iraqi Jews before the exodus of the 1950s were mainly from the upper and middle classes and were generally better off than the rest of the population, there were social and cultural gaps between different Jewish groups. These mirrored (albeit to a lesser extent) the cleavages in Iraqi society between urban and rural areas and between different Iraqi districts. Na'im Kattan (1976, pp. 40, 129), an Iraqi Jewish writer now living in Canada, recalls, for instance, that in Baghdad there were separate slum quarters inhabited by poor Jewish families of Kurdish origin. He has described how some of the wealthy Jewish families, including his own, employed girls from these quarters as servants.

---

1. The percentage of rural dwellers among the Kurdish Jews in the middle of the nineteenth century was greater than in 1947, while figures for rural dwellers among the Jews in southern and central districts as offered by the 1947 census need to be looked at more cautiously (see Table 2). Some Jews were not permanent residents but were there in connection with their jobs. This is shown by the fact that the majority of Jews in the rural areas of these districts were men.

Table 2: Jews in Iraq by Place of Residence, 1947

	Kurdish areas (Mosul & Kirkuk Districts)		Other Districts		Total
	Urban	*Rural*	*Urban*	*Rural*	*Total*
Male	5222	1312	52568	862	59964
Female	5527	1393	50657	459	58036
Total	10749	2705	103225	1321	118000
Rural population as percentage of whole		20.1		1.2	3.5

Source: Cohen (1973, p. 75), based on figures given in 1947 census, Ministry of Social Affairs, Baghdad, 1954, minor corrections inserted.

Cohen (1966b, p. 205) divides Iraqi Jews into three categories:

1. The Jews of Baghdad and Basra, who in 1950 constituted about 75 per cent of the total Iraqi Jewish population and who had begun to experience an improvement in economic and cultural conditions before the first world war.
2. The Jews of Kurdistan, some of whom began to migrate south to the main cities during the first half of this century. The overwhelming majority, however, remained scattered in villages and small towns and experienced no amelioration in their economic and educational conditions.
3. The small Jewish communities outside Kurdistan, which in 1950 made up some 15 per cent of Iraqi Jews and were able only after the first world war to benefit from the establishment of a few educational and health centres.

Educational and Cultural Integration

Urban Jews, who were influenced by contacts with the outside world, had a better chance of modern education than most other Iraqis. Jewish educational prospects were improved by the introduction of Alliance Israelite Schools by Alliance Israelite Universelle of Paris and by the strong communal spirit, which helped to establish more than one educational and vocational-training centre through donations from prominent members of the community who made their fortunes from trade abroad (the Sassoons and the Kadouries, for example).

The first Alliance School for boys was founded in Baghdad in 1865, and for girls in 1893. More elementary schools were later opened in the provincial towns. These schools brought modern methods of learning and included foreign languages in the curriculum alongside Arabic (French, English, and Turkish). After the British occupation, Alliance graduates provided the first nucleus of government clerical employees.

The economic position of the Iraqi Jews improved steadily after the first world war. The Jewish education system was strengthened, and by the 1920s numerous schools had been established, mostly by Jewish philanthropists, and were maintained by both Jewish community funds and regular contributions by the Iraqi government (Twena, 1975, pp. 69–71).

The number of schools supervised by the Jewish community in Baghdad continued to rise right up to the mass exodus of 1950–51. This is shown in Table 3 (below), which excludes pupils in non-Jewish schools, both government and private.

Even after the proclamation of Israeli statehood in 1948, new schools were still under construction. In his study of the education of the Jews in Iraq in the twentieth century, Itzhaki (1976) pointed out that of nine schools established by the community after Iraqi independence, six were built in the 1940s, including two in 1948–49. The total number of pupils attending these schools rose from 1,655 to 3,043 in the decade preceding 1949. Nine of ten subcommittees of the Community Educational Committee were formed in 1949.

In addition to normal schools, a number of other institutes were established. These included a school for the blind, orphanages, music schools, vocational centres, and charitable organizations.

Table 3: Schools Supervised by the Jewish Community in Baghdad

Year	Number of Schools	Number of Pupils	Budget in ID
1920	8	5511	–
1930	11	7182	22900
1935	12	7911	19700
1945	14	10021	57500
1949	20	10391	80300

Source: Cohen (1973, p. 123).

According to the chairman of the Iraqi Immigrants Organization in Israel, the community left thirty-seven institutes in Baghdad alone. These had been operated under its supervision and boasted a total of about twenty thousand students (quoted by Twena, 1975, p. 173).

Government schools were open to Jews as well as to other religious and ethnic minorities. When the Young Turks came to power in the Ottoman empire in 1908, modern schools for boys and girls were opened in Baghdad, along with a teacher-training college and a law school. A number of Jews were educated in these schools. Many joined Turkish colleges for education in medicine, law, pharmacy and engineering (Hilali, 1959, p. 208).

After independence the Iraqi government pursued an educational policy designed to reduce the differences between minorities in an attempt to achieve national unity. Through the 1930s more schools were established, the number of students in higher-education colleges mounted rapidly, and the number of Jews entering government schools increased.

In his volume on 'Jewish Education in Baghdad', Twena (1975, p. 170) pointed out that many Iraqi Jews preferred to send their children to government schools, primarily because they were free. During the 1940s, he explained, community schools provided mainly elementary education, while secondary education was mostly left to government schools. There were no restrictions on the number of Jewish students in government schools and colleges, although the preferential quota later introduced for scientific and medical colleges to favour a number of ethnic and religious groups may have adversely affected Jewish chances of entering these colleges. According to Itzhaki (1976), however, these quotas were never filled.

Jewish students started attending universities in Iraq and abroad after the first world war. Those leaving the country to study went mainly to Europe, the United States, Turkey, and India, as well as neighbouring Syria, Lebanon, and Egypt. No exact figures on how many completed their higher education are available. But there is enough evidence to suggest that the percentage of graduates among the Jewish community was far higher than for the rest of the population. The number of Jewish students sent abroad on government scholarships was also increasing. Itzhaki (1976) found that nearly half the total of those who went abroad on scholarships were Jewish.

A special research project of the Institute of Contemporary Jewry at the Hebrew University of Jerusalem (quoted by Cohen, 1973, pp. 124, 125) listed the names of Iraqi-born Jews who completed university education up to 1951. Although the list is not definitive, some interesting information may be gleaned from it. In the first half of this century about a thousand Jews completed their higher education: only 15 or so in the years 1901–10 compared to about 550 in 1940–50 (of whom 60 were women). In the year 1950 there were about 120 graduates (of whom 15 were women). In the first thirty years (1901–30) all graduates came from the major towns, Baghdad and Basra. Jews from smaller towns graduated only later. Finally, the main subject studied by Jews was law. Medicine came second, followed by pharmacy, engineering, and economics. Some joined teacher-training institutes and only a small number studied the humanities.

Some indication of the educational attainment of Iraqi Jews may be obtained from Israeli official statistics as presented in Table 4.

Table 4: Literacy Rates Among Middle Eastern Immigrants to Israel (in %)

Country of birth	Age at time of immigration				Median years of study
	15–29	*30–44*	*45–59*	*60+*	
Egypt and Sudan	94.7	90.2	75.6	62.1	–
Turkey	84.1	68.3	54.7	34.3	–
Syria and Lebanon	76	58.3	46.9	48.8	–
Iraq	69.5	52.9	39.2	27.8	–
Iran	63.7	47.2	31.5	23	–
Yemen and Aden	45	35.5	28.6	30.8	–
Men					
Egypt and Sudan	95.6	92.2	83.4	78.9	9.3
Turkey	89.4	79.4	71.3	56.6	6.6
Syria and Lebanon	87.2	83.4	68.8	71.7	–
Iraq	82.7	75.7	62.2	51.3	7.4
Iran	81.3	70.5	52.3	38.2	6.4
Yemen and Aden	74.5	64.5	56.3	57.1	6
Women					
Egypt and Sudan	93.9	–	–	–	–
Turkey	78.4	58.1	42.1	22.5	5.3
Syria and Lebanon	65	37.4	30.1	22.5	–
Iraq	56.1	28.5	14.2	6.8	2.9
Iran	46.5	21.5	8.4	3.2	1
Yemen and Aden	18.1	4.9	2.5	1.8	0.8

Source: Israeli Census 1961, No. 30, Tables 2, 8.

A number of conclusions may be drawn about literacy rates among Israeli immigrants from Islamic countries:

1. The Iraqi Jewish literacy rate was higher in the lower age group (between 15 and 59: 69.5 per cent) than among those over 60 (only 27.8 per cent).
2. There was a wide gap in the literacy rates for Iraqi Jewish men and women, especially among the elderly.
3. The literacy rate of Iraqi Jews was lower than that of Jews from Egypt, Turkey, Syria, and Lebanon, but higher than that of those from Iran or Yemen.
4. The overall literacy rate for all Iraqi Jewish immigrants generally exceeded 50 per cent at the time of the mass emigration. The overall Iraqi literacy rate in 1958 was only 15 per cent. As the literacy rate for all Iraqi Jews at the time of the mass emigration is unlikely to have been lower than that of emigrants to Israel,[1] it is safe to assume that the literacy rate among Israeli immigrants reflects a wide difference in educational standards between Iraqi Jews and the rest of the Iraqi population.

The founding of modern schools accelerated the secular, modern trend in education among Iraqi Jews, to the detriment of religious and traditional forms of education. The role of the *midrash* and *Yeshiva* was steadily undermined and became insignificant by the 1940s. The typical programme in the modern Jewish schools provided for instruction, in Arabic, in many subjects (languages, literature, science, geography, history, mathematics), with a greater emphasis on English than in government schools, many of which provided French as the prime second language and prepared pupils for French-administered examinations.

Modern education also paved the way for educated professionals to gain a greater say in running the community's affairs. Jews, like

---

1. Jews who remained in Iraq or left for countries other than Israel tended to be from the wealthiest sections of the community. Their literacy rate is unlikely to have been lower than that of emigrants to Israel.

other non-Muslims, administered their own communal affairs under the *millah* system.[1] There were two councils, one lay (or temporal) and one spiritual. Under Ottoman rule, these two councils derived their legal validity from an 1864 decree (or *irada*) by the sultan, later reinforced by Jewish community law no. 77 in 1931, under British rule. The lay council was known as al-Majlis al-Jismani and the spiritual as al-Majlis al-Ruhani (for more details see Sassoon, 1950).

The power of the spiritual council, which consisted of clergymen, diminished over time, its competence ultimately limited to matters relating to marriage, divorce, the attestation of wills, and the like. The lay council, whose members were elected every two years, was given power to administer civil matters such as education, health, and charities, as well as religious endowments and financial affairs. The lay council was empowered to levy taxes on the community and to administer the proceeds. Its principal sources of revenue were the *ghabilah* tax and a tax on meat.

From the late 1920s, leadership of the council was gradually assumed by educated professionals and intellectuals: lawyers, doctors, teachers, or merchants, who rejected the narrowness of the *mahallah* and sought closer integration with Iraqi society. Although they administered the community's affairs in a more liberal and enlightened manner, they continued to preserve the community's distinct identity.

The liberal and secular trends brought about a stronger association of Iraqi Jews and Arab culture. This in turn accelerated the process of cultural integration and brought Jews to a more active role in public and cultural life. A considerable number of prominent Jewish writers and poets emerged, whose works in Arabic were both highly regarded and well known. Among them were Me'ir Basri, the poet

---

1. Under this system, the *ahl al-kitab* ('people of the book'), which included only the Christians and Jews, had certain rights, including the right to worship and to administer their religious and civil affairs according to their own religious law. But Jews and Christians were required to pay the *jizya* (poll tax) in exchange for this protection under Islamic rule. This tax would be automatically revoked if the ruler failed to give them such protection.

Anwar Shaol, Murad Michael, Ya'coub Balbul, Salim Darwish and his brother Salman, Ibrahim Ya'coub, Ubaydah and Salim al-Katib, and Salim Kattan. Jewish intellectuals were among the first to begin translating books from other, mainly European, languages into Arabic.

A number of newspapers and magazines were founded by Jewish journalists. These included *al-Haris* (1920), *al-Misbah* (1924–29), *al-Hasad* (1929–37), *al-Bustan* (1929–38), *al-Barid al-Yawmi* (1948). All were in Arabic. Other Jewish journalists contributed to the local and Iraqi press and occasionally wrote for the Arabic press outside Iraq.

From the 1920s a number of Jews were also prominent in the Iraqi theatre and performed in Arabic. Many Jews in Iraq distinguished themselves in music, as they had in Turkey and Iran: as singers, composers, and players of traditional instruments. In his study of contemporary music in Iraq, Kojman (1978) mentions the names of at least 32 Jewish musicians among the top 100 musicians in Iraq.

The Jewish writers and artists of Iraq were in fact part of the general cultural life of the Arab East, maintaining connections and sometimes working relationships with writers and artists in other Arab countries. It is significant that in Iraq (unlike Lebanon, Egypt, or Tunisia for instance) there were few if any Hebrew or Zionist newspapers. The works of the Iraqi Jewish intelligentsia were Arabic in essence and expression.

Economic Assimilation

In the middle of the nineteenth century the majority of the Jews of Mesopotamia were engaged in crafts, hawking and small business (mainly in Baghdad), and agriculture (mainly in the Kurdistan region). More significantly, the Jewish community played a prominent role in finance and foreign trade. In 1879 a British consular report referred to the 'concentration of trade' in the hands of Jews in Baghdad (quoted by Batatu, 2004, p. 225). A similar assessment was given in a confidential account (known as the Shohet

Report) of the Jewish community of Baghdad, sent to Istanbul with marginal annotations by the British consul-general in Baghdad.[1] It stated: '… the Jews have literally monopolized the local trade and neither Mohammadans nor Christians can compete with them.'

The significant commercial role of the Jews may be attributed to a number of factors.

First, ownership of capital and the availability of credit enabled Jewish traders to gain a foothold in trade with Britain and assured their predominance among *sarrafs* (money lenders).[2] Their links with co-religionists and relatives in India, Europe, and elsewhere helped them to obtain credit. When they imported goods from India and England, they did so without the mediation of English merchants.

Second, the concentration of Jews in cities, especially Baghdad, and the migration of some (mainly to the Malabar coast, China, and England) helped them establish trading services and a communication network. Jewish migration to India dates back to the ninth century, but it was only after the abolition of the East India Company's trading monopoly that Baghdad's Jewish merchants went there in significant numbers. By the beginning of the twentieth century, nearly every important Baghdad merchant had subsidiary commercial houses in India or England. Ezra Sassoon, Haskail Shamash, Sha'ul Mu'allem Haskail, and Yahuda Zuluf all had houses in Manchester, while Sion Bikhor and Ezra Ishaq Salih had firms in both Bombay and London. Sir E. S. Kadourie had firms in Hong Kong, Shanghai, and London. In 1926 he became the vice-president of the Anglo-Jewish Association. But surpassing them all in wealth

---

1. The report was signed 'H. D. S.' These initials probably refer to Haron Da'ud Shohet, who was then employed as a dragoman at the British Consulate General (see Kedourie, 1971, pp. 355–61).
2. Among 39 listed *sarrafs* in Baghdad in 1936, 35 were Jews (Batatu, 2004, p. 250). Jews also established a number of banks during the British mandate, e.g. Zilkha Bank, Kradiyah Bank, Edward Aboodi Bank, and Kharith Bank (which established branches in several Middle Eastern countries including Egypt, Syria, and Lebanon). Zilkha Bank achieved some prominence in Iraq and was asked to transfer Iraq's contribution to the Arab League through its Cairo branch (see Ma'ruf, 1975, pp. 121–2).

and geographical diversification was the Sassoon family, often called the 'Rothschilds of the East' (Cecil, 1941).

Third, the growth of British (and other foreign) interests in Iraq had an impact on Jewish merchants. The country was being turned into an economic adjunct of the British empire, especially after the first world war. By 1919 as much as £5 million of British commercial capital was invested in Iraq. In the same year, imports from England accounted for almost two-thirds of Iraq's total imports by value. Most of this trade was conducted by Jewish merchants (for more details, see Batatu, 2004, p. 243).

As a result of the stronghold established by Jewish merchants, Muslim merchants became essentially intermediaries: they could compete neither against commission agents nor against English manufactured goods.

Between 1926 (when the Baghdad Chamber of Commerce was founded) and the late thirties British and mixed Anglo-French or Anglo-French-American companies constituted a majority of the Chamber's 'First Class' members (those whose capital was between 22,500 and 75,000 Iraqi dinars). Only one Arab Muslim belonged to this class.[1]

Of the twenty-five First Class members of the Chamber in 1938–39, no fewer than 10 were Jewish; 215 members (or 43 per cent of the total Chamber membership of 498) were Jewish (see Table 5). Baghdadi Jews thus constituted the largest mercantile group both numerically and in terms of wealth.

Although the commercial ascent of the Jews coincided with the expansion of British interests, it would be wrong to see this as entirely in accord with British desires. While they did help each other, Jewish and British traders were also competitors. This became clearer as the well-established Jewish merchants traded largely on their own accounts, while the British preferred to deal through commission agents or to have a direct share in the local trade.

---

1. Baghdad Chamber of Commerce, Annual Report for 1937–38, pp. 166–7 (quoted by Batatu, 2004, p. 246).

Table 5: Composition of Baghdad Chamber of Commerce, Financial Year 1938–39

Class of membership	First	Second	Third	Fourth	Fifth	Sixth	Total
Financial consideration[a] maximum limit in dinars[b]	75000	22500	7500	2250	375	100	
Total no. of members[c]	25	22	84	130	162	75	498
British	12	3	5	1	2	–	23
Other Western	2	–	2	3	2	–	9
Iraqi Jewish	7	11	44	73	58	19	212
Other Jewish	3[f]	–	–	–	–	–	3
Iraqi Arab Muslim Sunni	1	1	8	15	39	17	81
Iraqi Arab Muslim Shi'i	–	2[g]	11	17	33	24	87
Iraqi Kurd Muslim Sunni	–	–	2	–	–	4	6
Iraqi Christian[d]	–	2	6	12[j]	18	5	43
Iraqi Sabean	–	–	–	–	4	5	9
Arab other than Iraqi	–	3[h]	4	2	5	1	15
Others	–	–	2[i]	7[k]	1[l]	–	10

a. The financial consideration of each member was determined by the administrative committee of the Chamber in the light of the member's capital and volume of business and such other facts and circumstances as the committee deemed fit to take into account.
b. One dinar equalled one pound sterling.
c. Membership included companies and individual merchants and tradesmen.
d. Includes Armenians.
e. One British-French and one British-French-American-Armenian.
f. One French Jewish and two British Jewish.
g. Includes one mixed Shi'i-Sunni company.
h. Includes one merchant of mixed Syrian-Turkish parentage.
i. Persian Shi'is.
j. Includes one mixed Christian-Jewish concern.
k. Three Persians and four Indians.
l. Indian.

Source: Baghdad Chamber of Commerce, Annual Report for 1938/39, pp. 166–85 (quoted by Batatu, 2004, p. 245).

The British administration, on the other hand, created new employment opportunities for educated Jews, who were better qualified than others for the new civil service jobs. Many of them worked as senior clerks for the British advisers, who relied on them because of their greater familiarity with the country and its inhabitants.

The Iraqi Jews were therefore prominent in the civil service (especially in the treasury), transport, banks, and foreign companies. The majority of employees in the railways, the port of Basra, and the Iraq Petroleum Company, for example, were Jews. Perhaps the leading Jewish figure in the 1920s was Sassoon Hakim Haskail (Sir Sassoon Haskail), one of the eight members of the first government appointed by Sir Percy Cox (the British high commissioner in Iraq) and the first minister of finance.[1]

The Jews retained their prominence in the civil service after independence, mainly because of the rapid development of public services and the continuing presence of the British advisers. It was only when graduates among Muslims and other minorities began to compete for jobs and more Jewish professionals turned to running their own businesses that the Jewish role in the civil service started to wane. But the Jews kept their relative prominence in the treasury, the oil industry, the post office, and the railways.

Under the monarchy (1932–58) Iraq saw a rapid growth in the size of the middle class. Indicative of this is the rising number of traders with annual incomes of more than 150 dinars (from 1,862 in 1932–33 to 5,445 in 1942–43). The state administrative machine grew apace after independence. Government officials (excluding employees of the port and railways) numbered only 3,143 in 1920.

---

1. Names of other senior civil servants were listed by Ben-Ya'acov (1965, pp. 235–6), among them: Yitzhak Yehezkel Haim, who held a senior post in the Justice Department; Ibrahim al-Kabir, who was an under-secretary at the Ministry of Finance; Salim Tarzi, an under-secretary at the Ministry of Communications; Moshe Shohet, an assistant to the general director of the railways; Danod Samra, deputy to the head of the Court of Appeals; Ezra Eliahu, assistant manager of the Bureau of Public Affairs.

By 1938 that figure had risen to 9,740. The administrative and technical staff of the railways, on the other hand, rose from 1,639 in 1927 to only 1,738 a decade later (Batatu, 2004, p. 331).

This phenomenon is more marked in the case of the Jewish community, and is seen in the rising provision and level of their education, their predominance in the civil service, their commercial success, and the increasing number of those engaged in the professions. These changes were accompanied by the demographic shifts within the community and the migration from provincial areas to major urban centres.

The Shohet Report of 1910 categorized the community as follows: 5 per cent rich and well-off classes (consisting almost entirely of merchants and bankers), 30 per cent middle class (consisting of petty traders, retail dealers, and employees), 60 per cent poor and 5 per cent beggars.

By the 1940s the social structure had changed considerably. Although no precise figures are available, some inferences can be drawn from data published in Israel on the occupational composition of the Iraqi immigrants who had arrived in the country by 1951 (see Table 6). It should be remembered that the data cover about 90 per cent of the Iraqi Jewish community. The remaining 10 per cent did not migrate to Israel and probably had a far higher proportion of professionals, rich merchants, and officials than those who did. The richer layers remained in Iraq or left for other destinations (like Iran and Europe).

Table 6: Original Occupations of Israeli Immigrants, 1951

	BORN IN ASIA									
	Asia		Turkey		Iraq		Iran		Afghanistan	
	M	F	M	F	M	F	M	F	M	F
Total	23252	1899	316	46	20253	1651	1895	109	258	6
Professional and technical:	1167	310	20	7	1018	272	82	9	8	–
Medicine	264	161	9	4	221	138	23	6	1	–
Education	400	141	5	2	365	130	24	3	1	–
Engineering	181	1	2	–	148	–	22	–	1	–

	BORN IN ASIA									
	Asia		Turkey		Iraq		Iran		Afghanistan	
	M	F	M	F	M	F	M	F	M	F
Administrative and clerical	3502	95	33	5	3383	64	38	1	2	–
Commerce	6848	37	61	1	6180	34	412	–	81	–
Agriculture	1085	46	20	–	688	39	314	5	26	–
Mines and quarries	–	–	–	–	–	–	–	–	–	–
Transport	575	1	10	–	469	1	74	–	1	–
Crafts and industry:	6447	1052	90	25	5747	922	385	77	44	2
Clothing	1506	994	20	21	1368	887	87	62	10	1
Unskilled workers	2205	45	33	5	1621	33	404	3	84	1
Building	425	3	12	–	299	2	106	1	3	–
Personal services	867	299	28	2	743	277	65	11	8	3
Not specified	131	11	9	1	105	7	15	2	1	–

	BORN IN EUROPE OR AMERICA						BORN IN AFRICA					
	Europe & America		Poland		Romania		Africa		Libya		Tunisia, Algeria & Moroccco	
	M	F	M	F	M	F	M	F	M	F	M	F
Total	13392	2670	1162	290	10421	1675	4766	1008	1372	58	2821	789
Professional and technical:	1272	548	216	84	617	205	138	69	24	12	72	29
Medicine	252	227	54	37	51	86	22	47	2	11	5	22
Education	137	154	24	20	66	51	46	20	14	1	22	7
Engineering	270	48	52	13	90	20	17	–	1	–	10	–
Administrative and clerical	2282	447	156	40	1865	242	326	82	64	3	83	35
Commerce	3003	65	178	7	2478	47	643	20	258	2	325	12
Agriculture	876	116	45	9	660	16	426	107	56	–	290	80
Mines and quarries	3	–	1	–	–	–	1	–	–	–	–	–
Transport	463	4	50	–	375	3	123	–	19	–	85	–
Crafts and industry:	3080	821	422	118	2236	581	2255	620	562	15	1563	561
Clothing	683	718	111	104	518	511	440	533	131	9	288	482
Unskilled workers	1705	526	34	16	1625	494	368	29	208	8	131	15
Building	340	5	27	1	274	4	267	2	83	1	166	–
Personal services	315	125	26	14	261	75	176	68	82	17	88	46
Not specified	53	13	7	1	33	8	43	11	16	–	21	11

Source: Sicron (1957, p. 75).

Table 6 shows that:

The percentage of those engaged in professional and technical occupations among the Iraqi immigrants was almost the same (5.8 per cent) as the average for Asian communities as a whole, less than the corresponding percentage for the European and American communities (11.3 per cent), and higher than that of the African communities (3.6 per cent).

A high percentage (28.4) of the Iraqi immigrants dealt in commerce. This was higher than for any other community.

The proportion of Iraqi immigrants who worked in medicine and education (3.8 per cent) was higher than that of any other oriental community, and higher than some European communities as well.

The proportion of Iraqi immigrants who had worked in agriculture (3.3 per cent) was less than that of any other group, including European immigrants (6.1 per cent).

The proportion of unskilled workers (7.5 per cent) was less than that of any other group, including the European and American communities (13.8 per cent).

The growing size of the Iraqi middle class had another effect on the Iraqi Jewish community as well. Muslims (mainly Shi'i) began to play a larger role in commerce, while more educated Muslims among the new generation began to compete for jobs in both the public and private sectors. In his study Schechtman (1960, pp. 89 and 104) found that the relative economic position of Iraqi Jews began to decline when the British mandate came to an end in 1932. He observed that whereas they were conducting 95 per cent of the trade in the country in 1914, this proportion had fallen to 85–90 per cent in 1933 and to 65–70 per cent in 1946. He went on to argue, however, that the Jewish community maintained a prominent position in the country's economy until the exodus.

The reduction in the Jewish share of trade does not necessarily mean a reduction in its size. On the contrary, Jewish trade grew during the thirties and forties in terms of capital invested and number of traders. The increase did not match the overall increase because a rising number of Muslim traders, mainly Shi'is, started to come into the picture. As Jewish merchants left, the Shi'i took their place in the Baghdad Chamber of Commerce (see Table 7).

Table 7: Composition of Administrative Committee of Baghdad Chamber of Commerce, Selected Years

Year	Total membership	Arab Sunnis	Arab Shi'is	Kurds	Jews	Christians	British
1935–36	18	4	2	1	9	–	2
1948–49	18	4	6	1	7	–	–
1950–51	18	6	9	1	2	–	–
1957–58	18	4	14	–	–	–	–

Source: Baghdad Chamber of Commerce, Annual Reports: 1935–36, p. 14; 1948–49, p. 25; 1950–51, p. 9; 1957–58, p. 10 (quoted by Batatu, 2004, p. 271).

TWO

The Colonial Legacy

The expanding colonial interests in the Arab East towards the late nineteenth and early twentieth centuries altered the position of minorities and introduced Zionism to the region.

The Colonial Approach to Minorities in the Arab East

British sources generally claim that the Iraqi Jewish community needed their protection when they took over Mesopotamia after the first world war. One British official, for example, Gertrude Bell, reported that the Iraqi Jews had asked for direct British rule (quoted by Kedourie, 1970, p. 300 ff.), while the British civil commissioner, Sir Arnold Wilson, writing in 1930, noted that Iraqi Jews had demanded guarantees of their 'lives, honour, and property' before giving their approval to the establishment of a provisional Arab government in October 1920.

It is reasonable to assume that the Jews, like other minorities, tended to keep on the right side of authority, be it Turkish or British. The Turks, for instance, consistently regarded the Jews as loyal subjects, and this may be one reason why the British replaced the chief rabbi of the Iraqi community directly after the occupation, on the grounds that he was pro-Turk (Twena, 1975, p. 7). It is also possible that some Jewish notables asked that the constitutional rights of their community be secured during the period of uncertainty that followed the collapse of Turkish rule and the establishment of an Arab government under British sponsorship.

It is wrong to assume, however, that Iraqi Jews as a community asked for direct British rule. Such views were most probably expressed by the upper layer of the Jewish trading class, which was the main beneficiary of the British presence. Similar views were also expressed by Muslim and Christian notables in a letter to the high commissioner in June 1921.[1]

It must be emphasized that nothing in the history of Jewish relations with the Turkish authorities justified a demand for British protection or direct rule. Indeed, Abraham Goalanté, a Jewish historian who researched the position of the Jewish communities under the Turks, concluded that Jews were far better treated in the Ottoman provinces than in Europe. Goalanté pointed out that after the outbreak of anti-Semitic manifestations towards the end of the nineteenth century, Turkey gave shelter to thousands of Jews fleeing persecution in Eastern Europe, allowing them to settle wherever they pleased (see Cohen, 1973, p. 18).

In fact, the issue of minorities in the Ottoman provinces grew in importance as the European colonial powers became more involved in the Arab East. The Capitulation system granted certain privileges – including exemption from certain taxes and local laws – to nationals of some European countries and some minorities. The implementation of the Capitulation system and the protection accorded foreigners and some minority groups gave the colonial powers a foothold in the area and accelerated the decline of Turkish rule. France, for example, claimed the right to protect Catholics and Maronites, while Russia extended its protection to the Greek Orthodox population. Since there was no Anglican presence in the area, Britain sought to become the protector of the Druze and was the first to appreciate the role of the Jewish communities.

This interest in Jewish communities was probably motivated by the commercial role of the Jews. Moreover, London was beginning

---

1. Report from the High Commission for Mesopotamia (Cox) to the Secretary of State for the Colonies, 11th June 1921, co 730/2/34955.

to show interest in finding an extra-European solution to the 'Jewish Question'. It was thought that a European Jewish presence in the Arab East might support British interests in the area and simultaneously solve the problem of Jewish immigration to Britain (see Khalidi, 1971, pp. 97–114).

Towards the end of the nineteenth century a number of schemes to settle European Jews in the Arab East were floated in British circles. Various areas were discussed, such as southern Mesopotamia and al-Arish in Sinai (see Grobba, 1967). But these schemes met with Turkish opposition and were not pursued. More efforts were made to settle Jews in Palestine after the emergence of Zionism as a political movement in 1897. This was backed by some European colonial powers, but it soon became clear that the Turkish authorities were as opposed to the new scheme as they had been to the previous ones.

But the political scene in the Arab East changed dramatically in the aftermath of the first world war. As the Turks pulled out and the British and French stepped in, the scope for Zionist activities widened. Between the two world wars Zionist activities were allowed, but Zionist freedom of action and influence in the various Jewish communities of the Arab East differed, depending on the extent of European influence and the size of the European Jewish presence. In Egypt, for example, where a large number of European Jews lived, Zionist activities were officially permitted until the late 1940s. By contrast, in countries like Syria and Iraq, where there were few European Jews and the nationalist movement was more alert to the danger, the Zionists kept a low profile, conducting their activities less openly.

Zionism Versus the Orient

The development of Zionism was a response to the anti-Semitism that spread through Eastern Europe in the nineteenth century. Abraham Leon (1970) offered an acute analysis of the socio-economic factors that stimulated anti-Semitism in Europe and subsequently the emergence of the 'Jewish Question'. Leon wrote:

> The highly tragic situation of Judaism in our epoch is explained by the extreme precariousness of its social and economic position. The first to be eliminated by decaying feudalism, the Jews were also the first to be rejected by the convulsions of dying capitalism. The Jewish masses find themselves wedged between the anvil of decaying feudalism and the hammer of rotting capitalism … (p. 226)

Zionism, which arose as one of the answers to the Jewish Question, thus remained a European phenomenon, and the factors that led to its emergence were almost wholly absent in the Orient, where medieval conditions prevailed until recently (see Rodinson, 1983). Zionism was founded on the concept of Jewish national unity and called for the establishment of a Jewish state. Its success was partly due to the support of the colonial powers, who viewed its project as potentially useful to Western interests. The founder and leading theoretician of Zionism, Theodor Herzl, made this promise in 1896: 'For Europe we shall serve there as vanguard of civilization against the barbarians.' (Quoted by Shapiro, 1978.)

Separate ethnic and religious groups existed in the Orient, but common cultural factors prevailed. The Jews in Islamic countries lived as a religious entity: their communal life had almost the same cultural and social features as that of their non-Jewish compatriots (for more discussion, see Rodinson, 1983). Even after the emergence of Arab nationalism near the end of the last century, there is no evidence to suggest that indigenous Jewish communities in the Arab world saw themselves as a national entity.

The cultural and social gap between the indigenous Jews of the Orient and the European Jews who settled in Islamic countries was as wide as that which divided Islamic and European societies. An Egyptian Jewish writer recently wrote:

> The Jewish community in Egypt was divided intellectually, physically, and emotionally. One part clung to a struggle which quickly became a rearguard battle to maintain its Egyptian identity. The other part succumbed to foreign powers and thus contributed to its own material and intellectual liquidation ... (Eskandarany, 1978, p. 29)

The Zionists seem to have viewed the indigenous oriental Jews as a reserve work-force to be imported when required. In a report to the Palestine Office of the Zionist movement in 1908, Dr J. Thorn suggested that one solution to the shortage of labour in the Jewish settlements was the use of 'indigent oriental Jews, who are still on the same cultural level as the Arab fellahin' (quoted by Bein Alex, 1970, p. 97). This suggestion came at a time when the second wave of European settlers could stand neither the hardship and toil of manual labour nor the inhospitable climate of Palestine, and the Zionist enterprise seemed in grave danger. Two years later, the Zionists imported several thousand Yemeni Jews to work as agricultural labourers in Palestine. In the 1920s and 1930s young men were also brought from Jewish communities in India, Morocco (the Atlas mountains), and Kurdistan to work in settlements around Tiberias and other particularly hot areas in the Jordan valley and southern Palestine.

This engendered another problem for those who saw Zionism as an answer to the problems of East European rather than oriental Jews. The European Zionists believed that the rising number of oriental Jews would affect the 'quality' of the entire Jewish community in Palestine (called the Yishuv). In an article published in the spring of 1912, Ahad Ha'am, a shrewd Jewish thinker who remained sceptical of political Zionism, made these remarks:

> Of late, Jews have been arriving in Palestine from Yemen, and have been settling in the colonies and working there as labourers ... whereas their entire mentality is so different from ours, that the question automatically arises whether by their increase the quality of the whole Yishuv may not change

and whether the change would be for the better (Ha'am, 1947, p. 426).

Meanwhile, the more developed and established communities among the oriental Jews – in Turkey, Iraq, and Egypt – were sceptical about Zionism, and most of their thinkers engaged in active opposition to the Zionist movement. The Jews of Istanbul, regarded as the most enlightened of these communities, were involved in anti-Zionist activities by the same year that the world Zionist movement was founded. They published a newspaper, *al-Masrant* (1897–1919), which warned against Zionism (Cohen, 1976, pp. 38–47).

In fact, Zionist activities among the oriental Jews were led by Europeans who showed a striking lack of understanding of these communities. Both Cohen (1969, 1976) and Chouraqui (1968) listed the language barrier and lack of understanding on the part of the Zionist activists among the main factors hindering the promotion of Zionist ideals among the oriental communities. Cohen (1969) rightly considered the British presence as the main factor behind Zionist activities in Iraq after the first world war. In March 1921 Sir Percy Cox, the British high commissioner, granted the Jam'iyya al-Sahyuniyya li-Bilad al-Rafidain (Mesopotamian Zionist Committee) permission to operate. Two years later permission was officially withdrawn, but the Committee nevertheless continued its activities through British and other European Jews who had lived in Iraq for various periods. They appear to have established contact with some local Jews in order to collect contributions for the Keren-Kaymeth (Jewish National Fund) and Keren-Haysod (Palestine Foundation Fund).

Documents of the Zionist Archive examined by Cohen (1969) showed that fund-raising was the principal objective of the Zionists in Iraq during the 1920s. The size of contributions increased during the early years of British rule (1920–24), but declined steadily afterwards, and Iraqi Jews were not represented at any international Zionist Congress after 1927. Evidence also shows that Congress representatives of the community before that date were actually foreigners who had succeeded in selling in Iraq the number of 'shekels' required for representation by Zionist Congress rules.

Although Zionist emissaries were well received and helped by the mandate authorities and senior Iraqi officials, Iraqi Jews seemed largely indifferent and often hostile. When the Zionist Committee was given permission to function, a special delegation headed by community leaders met with the British high commissioner to express their opposition.[1] The Zionists failed to attract any influential community figures and their activities were mainly carried out by one local Jew who lacked influence and was described by the Zionist organization itself as a 'failed teacher' whose honesty was suspect (Cohen, 1969, p. 36). He was later expelled to Palestine at the request of community leaders (Darwish, 1981, p. 33).

On one of the anniversaries of the Balfour Declaration, Sir Arnold Wilson wrote to the Colonial Office assessing the reaction to the declaration in Iraq:

> The announcement aroused no interest in Mesopotamia, nor did it leave a ripple on the surface of local political thought in Baghdad, where there had been for many centuries a large Jewish population whose relations with Arabs had caused them far less concern than the attitude of their Turkish rulers. I discussed the declaration at the time with several members of the Jewish community, with whom we are on friendly terms. They remarked that Palestine was a poor country and Jerusalem a bad town to live in. Compared with Palestine, Mesopotamia was Paradise. This is the Garden of Eden, said one; it is from this country that Adam was driven forth – give us a good government and we will make this country flourish. For us Mesopotamia is a home, a national home to which the Jews of Bombay and Persia and Turkey will be glad to come. Here shall be liberty and opportunity. In Palestine, there may

---

1. According to Nuri al-Said, the meeting took place without the knowledge of the Iraqi authorities (see Rawi, 1977).

be liberty but there will be no opportunity (Wilson, 1930, pp. 305–06).

Indeed, the views of some influential figures in the community were critical of Zionist tactics or ideology. An example of the first is offered by Menahem Saleh Daniel, a Baghdadi notable and landowner. In a letter to the World Zionist Organization (WZO) in 1922 responding to a request for help in promoting Zionist activities in Iraq, Daniel foresaw danger to the community because of the style of politics that Zionism endorsed. He wrote:

> The Jews are already acting with culpable indifference to public and political affairs, and if they espouse so publicly and tactlessly as they have done lately a cause which is regarded by the Arabs not only as foreign but as actually hostile, I have no doubt that they will succeed in making themselves a totally alien element in this country, and as such, they will have great difficulty in defending a position, which … is on other grounds already too enviable. (Quoted by Khaddouri, 1971, p. 357.)

Zionist ideology was attacked by another prominent figure, Yusuf al-Kabir, a Baghdadi Jewish lawyer, in a letter published in the *Iraq Times* on 5 November 1938. Al-Kabir declared that 'the problem which the Balfour Declaration purported to solve was, and remained, a European problem, both by origin and present incidence.' He went on: 'The Declaration was a very risky piece of political acrobatics', a scheme 'founded on a manifestly unworkable partnership'.

In discussing the difficulties Zionism was bound to encounter in Palestine, al-Kabir took up the absurdities of the nationalist argument. He commented on the idea that Jews could lay claim to Palestine now because the country was theirs two thousand years ago, writing:

Reconstruction of historical geography, if accepted as a practical theory, would for instance bring the case of Ulster to ground, and provide a recognized legal basis for German claims on Eastern Europe. In a certain influential section of the German press, the theory is now being held out that Eastern Europe, up to the Volga, was in some remote time wholly occupied by Germans. If the legal basis is accepted, there remains nothing but to work out history in detail for a suitable epoch, and everyone knows that modern science can do anything. Moreover, if one goes reconstituting history two thousand years back, there is no reason why one should not go still further back, say four or five thousand years, and presently have the world ruled by militant archaeology.

Before 1948 there was insignificant emigration from Iraq to Palestine. The little migration that occurred was mostly for religious reasons. The international economic crisis in the late 1920s and the promulgation of the military service law in 1934 probably led to some further emigration. No precise figures are available, but rough estimates offered by Cohen (1969, pp. 109–12), based on figures drawn up mainly by the Jewish Agency and the mandate authorities in Palestine, put the number at about 8,000 (see Table 8).

Table 8: Iraqi Jewish Immigrants to Palestine 1919–48

Year	Number
1919–23	171
1924–31	3290
1932–38	2927
1939–45	1532
1946–48	65
Total	7995

Bearing in mind that a considerable number of those who emigrated were of Kurdish origin (some estimates suggest that about five thousand Kurdish Jews left Iraq in the thirties with the help of the Jewish Agency)[1] and that some of those registered as immigrants may have died or left Palestine after their arrival, these figures of Iraqi immigrants are probably exaggerated. In fact in 1948 more Baghdadi Jews could be found in India, where up to that year they maintained a flourishing community of about 6,500 (Shaloah, 1976, p. 63).

Iraqi Nationalists in the 1920s[2]

British rule under the mandate in Iraq applied two common colonial principles. Ethnic and religious divisions among the population were exploited to the maximum, and a pro-British, relatively powerless, local government was set up. The diverse ethnic and religious origin of the Iraqi population made it easier to operate the first principle. In the early stage of the British occupation, for instance, promises were made to the Kurds and Assyrians, while the mandate authorities seemed more than willing to exploit longstanding British commercial ties with the Jews. The British civil commissioner wrote in 1918: 'The elements that we most need to encourage are, firstly, the Jewish community in Baghdad' (quoted by Batatu, 2004, p. 311).

On the other hand, the British soon embarked on a policy of backing a pro-British provisional government, established under Sunni domination. They devised a system of control which, as Sluglett noted in the preface to his *Britain in Iraq* (1976),

> could be exercised as unobtrusively and cheaply as possible. With limited resources, but with a long tradition of colonial administration behind them, the British authorities built up a

---

1. See Fishel us 'Sinai', Vol. VII, uncertain date, pp. 968–94.
2. The term 'nationalist' is used throughout to denote the national movement. It should not be taken to refer only to Arab nationalism or pan-Arabism, since it includes other forces such as national democrats, religious opposition, and Communists. Thus 'nationalism' as used here encompasses two Arabic words: *watani* (national) and *qawmi* (nationalist).

system based on a subtle mixture of cajolery, blandishment, and bluff. In these circumstances, where Britain had the upper hand, but could not afford too frequent or too clumsy displays of her superiority, the creation of a basically loyal if occasionally restive political authority in Iraq was vital.

Many Iraqi nationalists viewed the privileged position that some ethnic and religious minorities enjoyed under British rule as part of the colonial legacy, which only helped to foster prejudice and animosity. The achievement of equality became an inseparable part of their struggle for freedom and independence, and of their determination to put an end to British domination. Further, when the British found it more suitable to consolidate the authority of the central government, they reneged on the pledges they had originally given to some ethnic and religious minorities. The Kurds rebelled against the central government, demanding autonomy. The Assyrians, after first being recruited and used by the British to put down major (Kurdish and Arab) anti-British uprisings, were later violently suppressed by the Iraqi army (in 1933). The Baghdadi Jews were also subjected to unprecedented acts of violence in June 1941, as we shall see later.

Hourani (1947, p. 94) attributed these violent incidents to what he called 'the amorphous nature' of the state of Iraq and not to 'bad will' on the part of either the majority or the minorities. Hourani's interpretation highlighted the vulnerability of Iraqi society but failed to see it as one consequence of the traditional colonial approach pursued by the British.

At least until the 1920s, nationalists regarded the Jews as brothers and comrades. In an earlier phase, Arab nationalists (or at least most of them) considered the Jews of the Arab countries as an indivisible part of the Arab 'race'. A manifesto issued by the Arab Revolution Committee in 1915, two years before the Balfour Declaration, appealed in these terms to 'Arabs of the Christian and Jewish faith': 'Join ranks with your Muslim brethren. Do not listen to those who say that they prefer the Turks without religion to Arabs of different beliefs; they are ignorant people who have no understanding of the vital interest of the race' (quoted by Batatu, 2004, p. 258).

Years after the end of Turkish rule, when they were involved in yet another struggle, this time against the British, the Iraqi nationalists still viewed the Jews among them as brothers and companions. Evidence recently brought to light by Khalid 'Abd al-Muhsin (1983), based mainly on Colonial Office papers, shows that both the nationalist leadership and the religious leaders (the *'ulema*) were urging Muslims to unite their political and social activities with their Jewish and Christian compatriots during the major anti-British uprising of 1920.

When rumours spread that the lives of Jews and Christians were in danger 'because of their pro-British stance', Ja'far Abu'l-Timman, one of the most prominent nationalist leaders during the uprising and through the 1920s, acted swiftly to allay their fears and to bring the different groups together. Leaflets were sent to leading Jews and Christians and distributed in coffee shops frequented by non-Muslims. 'To all our Brothers, Christian and Jewish fellow citizens', one of the leaflets read,

> It is to be made clear to you, our brothers, that we in this country are partners in happiness and misery. We are brothers and our ancestors lived in friendship and mutual help. Do not consider in any way that the demonstrations carried out by the citizens affect any of your rights. We continue to value and respect our friendship. All demonstrations being made do not indicate a lack of respect for you or any citizen. We have no other object than to claim from the present government the fulfilment of its pledges in the newspapers to the Iraqi nation. We therefore invite you to take part with us in everything that is good for the nation. Be assured that our union and mutual support will be illustrious in the future of our fatherland on which our common happiness depends. We again invite you in the name of the fatherland and patriotism to unite, in order to form a single land to work for the realization of our principles and our future happiness

whereby you will render us thankful to you. (Quoted by 'Abd al-Muhsin, 1983, pp. 269–70.)

When acts of violence erupted in Palestine in the late 1920s, the Iraqi nationalists set up a Protest Committee (PC) on Palestine. Public meetings and demonstrations were organized against the Zionists and the British, especially when a prominent Zionist, Alfred Mond (later Lord Melchett), visited Baghdad in February 1928. The response was government repression. Force was used to disband meetings and many students were arrested. According to CID reports, the British officials played the major role in suppressing the public feeling on Palestine at the time, and the activities of the PC were gradually brought to an end.[1]

British CID reports also show unequivocally that Ja'far and his fellow nationalists made their views on Palestine very clear at the time: the question of Palestine 'would amount to confrontation with the British authorities in Iraq as well as with their Arab allies in the region'; the Iraqi Jews were not similar to the new Jewish settlers in Palestine. They rather blamed 'the Jews from Russia, Germany and other European countries' for what was happening in Palestine.[2]

Several Baghdadi Jews joined ranks with Muslims and Christians in denouncing the British policy in Palestine. On 1 September 1919 telegrams were sent by certain Jews to *al-Iraq* and *al-Nahda* newspapers declaring support for the Arab stand against the Balfour Declaration.[3] When the nationalists organized a meeting in Haider Khana Mosque on 13 September 1929, a large crowd including Muslims, Christians, and Jews from all social groups listened to speeches from Ja'far and other nationalist leaders blaming Britain for supporting the Zionist scheme in Palestine and accusing the Iraqi

---

1. 'Top Secret' Memorandum from the Ministry of the Interior to 'All Administrative Inspectors for Iraq', 12th September 1929, No. CO/3036/17 (quoted by Abd al-Muhsin, 1983, p. 270).
2. C.I.D. 'Secret' Report No. S.B.400, 20 August 1929, file No. 16/78 in N.A.I., New Delhi, CO/1983 (quoted by Abd al-Muhsin, 1983, pp. 198–252).
3. C.I.D. 'Secret' Report, 14 September 1929, No. S.B.435, file no. 7/17/144, in N.A.I., New Delhi (quoted by Abd al-Muhsin, 1983, pp. 253–340).

government of being subject to foreign influence. Anwar Shaol, a Jewish poet and a friend of Ja'far, attributed the trouble in Palestine to British colonial policy and said that the Balfour Declaration 'was designed to further imperialist ambitions'. Speakers declared frequently that they were against Zionism, not Judaism.[1]

The Power Struggle After Independence

The end of the British mandate in November 1932 brought official independence but few major changes. The pro-British ruling class remained intact, and a treaty of alliance with Britain cast doubt on the efficacy of independence. The treaty, which had been signed in 1930, was considered by the nationalists not only to have impeded the realization of Iraq's political aspirations, but also as inimical to social and economic development (for more details, see Khadduri, 1951, pp. 311–12). Iraq under the monarchy witnessed a notable new rise of an urban middle class as a result of economic development stimulated by the increase in oil revenues and the expansion of public sectors and services (see al-Samarra'i, 1973, p. 138, and Gabbay, 1978). Two contradictory processes were taking place: while the socio-economic transformation and the formation of social classes had accelerated, the monarchy generally clung to the structure and practices of the old system inherited from the British.

The struggle between the newly emergent social classes (with their demands for national sovereignty, termination of the 1930 treaty with Britain, and freedom and democratic rights) and the ruling class became the main factor in Iraq's political life under the monarchy. In the absence of democratic outlets, opposition sometimes expressed itself in other ways. There were tribal rebellions, urban uprisings, and strikes. Two urban uprisings caused the fall of cabinets in 1948 and 1952; another, in 1956, proved abortive.

---

1. Ibid.

On each occasion a state of emergency was introduced and severe restrictions imposed. Al-Hasani (1964, p. 351) pointed out that Iraq under the monarchy spent more time than not under emergency rule. He listed sixteen instances between 1920 and 1958 in which a state of emergency was imposed. These brought the army onto the political scene at an early stage in the history of independent Iraq. It was the first experience of this kind in the Middle East, and led some officers to consider the coup as a means of effecting political changes. A coup led by General Bakr Sidqi brought down the government in October 1936. Four years later, in April 1941, another coup led by four colonels installed Rashid Ali al-Gailani as prime minister and precipitated the flight and eventual deposition of the pro-British regent, who, with British encouragement, sought to remove al-Gailani.

For most of the period of monarchy, two branches of the nationalist movement can be discerned: the national democrats and the pan-Arabists. Both sought to put an end to British domination. The democrats[1] gave more emphasis to democratic rights and social reforms, while the pan-Arabists stressed the achievement of Arab unity and were less tolerant of ethnic and national minorities. This division became more acute over time and was later to polarize the political scene in Iraq. The democratic branch was represented during the thirties by the al-Ahali group, which played a prominent role at the time and at one point entered a fragile coalition with Sidqi (1936–37) during which the country witnessed its first short-lived period of liberalization and reform (al-Wakil, 1976). The pan-Arabist branch was represented by the al-Gailani movement, during whose period of rule (April–May 1941) Iraq became a hotbed of Arab nationalism. After the second world war the two branches were represented by the National Democratic Party and the Communists on the one hand and by the Istiqlal Party on the other.

---

1. The term 'democrat' will henceforth be used in the sense it holds in Middle Eastern and Iraqi politics: emphasis on democratic rights and political freedoms. This stance characterizes the left wing of the national movement and encompasses Communists and other leftist groups as well as the centre-left, represented by the National Democratic Party.

The al-Gailani movement gave rise to two sources of anxiety among Iraqi Jews. First, there was the emphasis on Palestine. The Palestine Question was assuming some prominence in Iraqi politics at both the official and the popular levels. Many Palestinian nationalists, including Haj Amin al-Husaini, found refuge in Iraq after the major anti-British uprising of 1936 in Palestine. Along with Syrian and Iraqi nationalists, they formed the Arab Committee, which later, in the months of April and May 1941, not only guided the destiny of Iraq but also sought the realization of Arab nationalist aspirations in Syria and Palestine. Salah al-Din al-Sabbagh, one of the four colonels who led the 1941 movement and who died on the gallows after its collapse, explained that one of the reasons behind the 1941 movement in Iraq was the government's failure to aid the Palestinian Arabs (see *Fursan al-Uruba*, 1956, pp. 119–20).

The source of anxiety was the attitude to Germany. Some Arab nationalists, like other nationalists in British colonies at the time, saw the second world war as an opportunity to put an end to foreign domination, with German help if necessary. Although it would be wrong to label the leadership of the national movement at the time as 'Nazi' – as most Zionist sources tend to do (see Cohen, 1969, for example), it is fair to assume that Nazi propaganda found some supporters in stirring up anti-Jewish feeling in Iraq.

There is no evidence that any serious harm was done to the Jews while al-Gailani was in power, but a few cases of harassment of individual Jews were brought to light (at a later stage) by the Communists, who had supported al-Gailani (Batatu, 2004, pp. 453–5). It was only after the collapse of the al-Gailani government that Baghdadi Jews suffered the first major act of violence. Given its unprecedented nature and the significance that the events of the 'Farhud' were to assume in the minds of many Iraqi Jews, a brief explanation of the sequence of events is necessary.

The al-Gailani government declared its intention to keep Iraq out of the war. This gave the British an excuse to reoccupy Iraq as part of their war strategy. The treaty of 1931 was served as justification. The regent, who had fled Baghdad, found shelter with British forces first in the Gulf and later in Amman, Jordan. British troops landed in Basra at the beginning of May 1941 and neared Baghdad by the end of the month. The nationalist leaders, recognizing that they had lost the battle, fled the country on 30 May. The British forces occupied strategic positions in the outskirts of Baghdad, and the regent returned to the capital on 1 June.

For two or three days there was a power vacuum in Baghdad. It was a critical period, full of tension, with emotions running high as the humiliated nationalists realized that they had lost the month-long fight with the British and their supporters. A riot erupted in the capital on 1 June and spread rapidly. Houses and stores were looted and some 250–300 people, mostly Jews, were killed or injured[1] in what is often called the Farhud (in Iraq this means 'breakdown of law and order').

An official investigation was conducted and the British version of the events was adopted. This held 'the nationalists and German propaganda responsible'. Many people were arrested and tried by military courts; three were publicly executed on 13 July 1941, and the government contributed £70,000 to the Jewish Relief Committee (Haim, 1978, pp. 194–5).

In their account of the events that led to the violence, both al-Hasani (1953) and Haim (1978) refer to expressions of joy openly displayed by groups of Jews at the news of the impending arrival of British troops and the return of the regent. This attitude was seen as provocative by the nationalists, who were in dismay after their defeat. It is doubtful that the expressions of joy were the only reason for the unprecedented violence that followed, but it seems to have provided the trigger. Haim (1978) stated that 'the prominent

---

1. An Official Investigation Committee put the number killed at 110 (including 28 Muslims), with 204 injured; the head of the Jewish community put the number killed at 130 (including 25 missing), with 450 injured. See full report of the Official Investigation Committee and estimates made by the head of the Jewish community in al-Hasani (1964, pp. 72–3). These figures are much lower, and probably more reliable, than other estimates, given mainly by Zionist sources. See, e.g., Twena (1977, pp. 111–16).

members of the community who always counselled caution and reserve were very worried about this display of joy' (p. 194).

Certainly many nationalists were suspicious and resentful of pro-British trends among the Jewish community. Al-Hasani (1964, p. 69) argued that rumours of Jewish collaboration with the British became popular beliefs in Baghdad before the collapse of the al-Gailani government. What might have given some credibility to such a view was the participation of Jewish military units from Palestine, under British command, in the fight against the nationalists (for more details see Sayyigh, 1966, pp. 26–83).

There are those who believe that the British were mainly responsible for the violence, as part of a policy of diverting public anger while completing their takeover of the country. In his collection Twena (1977, pp. 89–90) listed at least three incidents to support this view. A similar view was offered by Me'ir Basri, the head of the Iraqi Jewish community in the 1960s.[1] Cohen (1966, p. 8) suggested that the British turned a blind eye to similar acts of violence (although on a smaller scale) in two other towns, Basra and al-Falluja, where houses and shops were looted with no distinction made between Jewish and non-Jewish properties.

It is intriguing that no documents from June 1941 relevant to the violence of that month could be found among Foreign Office papers.[2] But there seems little doubt that the British were reluctant to intervene. This was confirmed by Freya Stark (1945), who was then a senior official at the British Embassy in Baghdad. She wrote: 'The British troops, encamped some miles from Baghdad, were anxious not to enter the town unless invited, and the Iraqi forces of law were equally anxious to win their own fight unaided' (p. 160).

This assessment of the British position was echoed by an intelligence officer with the British troops near Baghdad, who explained that the British and their allies among the Iraqi politicians were anxious not to undermine the standing of the regent by direct

---

1. In an interview with the author in London, 6 June 1981.
2. Woolfson (1980) mentions a document that remains closed on the grounds that it would not be in the public interest to release it until 2017.

interference in such a delicate situation (quoted by Me'ir, 1973, p. 63).

Economic conditions at the time may also have been a factor in the riots. Necessities were expensive and the poorest sections of the population could not afford them. Most of the looters seem to have been slum-dwellers around Baghdad. 'They came from the other side of the Tigris to loot and not to kill, and well-to-do areas were their target', was how Stark (1945) described them. The bridges connecting the two banks of Baghdad (al-Karkh and al-Rusafa), she wrote, 'were a strange sight, an empty-handed crowd going eastward and returning with arms overweighted with parcels of every sort' (p. 160). Stark estimated that sixty to seventy looters were killed when the regent ordered loyal Kurdish troops to enter the city, imposing a curfew and shooting on sight. Many Iraqis at the time blamed Jewish merchants and their powerful partners for shortages of food and goods, and for the speculation that followed the British recapture (al-Hasani, 1958, pp. 102–03, 195–6).

It is against this background of complex factors and exceptional events that the violence of 1941 took place. It is simplistic to see the Farhud as a fundamentally anti-Jewish act; it was rather the result of deep and suppressed anti-British feeling, which found its outlet against the Jews. Hirst (1977) puts it thus: 'On the rare occasions in Arab history when Muslims – or Christians for that matter – turned against the Jews in their midst, it was not anti-Semitism, in its traditional European sense, that drove them, but fanaticism bred of a not unjustified resentment.' He continues

> For like other minorities the Jews had a tendency to associate themselves with, indeed to profit from, what the majority regarded as an alien and oppressive rule. In recent times, this meant that from Iraq to Morocco, the local Jewish communities found varying degrees of special favour with the French or British masters of the Arab world. If Arab Jews must themselves take some of the blame for the prejudice which this behaviour generated against them, they deserve much less blame for that other cause of Arab hostility –

Zionism – which was ultimately to prove infinitely more disruptive of their lives (p. 161).

The Zionist Failure

The events of the Farhud had a deep psychological effect on the Iraqi Jews. The unprecedented violence shocked many into re-examining their relationship with other Iraqis, and seriously dented their feeling of security. But although these events became part of Jewish folklore, they seemed not to lead to any serious shift of opinion in favour of Zionism. It was only eight or nine years later that the experience of the Farhud was fully exploited.

There are indications, however, that Baghdadi Jews were soon able to overcome the trauma of 1941 and that the violence was apparently forgotten. One factor in this was the commercial boom during the war, of which the Jewish business community was the prime beneficiary. Many acted as contractors and suppliers for the British occupation forces (estimated at about one hundred thousand). The few families who had obtained visas to go abroad (mainly to live with relatives in India) soon changed their minds.[1] Zionist emissaries who arrived in Iraq during the war were struck by the lack of response on the part of Iraqi Jews. But the British presence did offer opportunities for Zionist activities. The presence of Jewish military units from Palestine as part of the British occupying force helped (for more details, see Me'ir, 1973, and Atlas, 1969). Ideal cover for Zionist emissaries was provided by Jewish contractors from Palestine working for the British in Iraq, like Solel Boneh, the construction company of the Histadrut, and Egged (Palestine Transport Company). Finally, some Zionists enjoyed a certain influence at the time through their commercial ties with Iraqi officials.

The main concern of the Zionists was to win over the European Jews who had fled during the war and found refuge in Arab

---

1. Baghdad to FO, 25 September 1941, FO 371/27116 87/29/41.

countries. David Kimche (1976, pp. 60–2) described how emissaries were sent to Arab countries and Europe to organize the transfer of Jews to Palestine. He noted that the Iraqi Jewish community, like their coreligionists in Egypt and Tunisia, were reluctant to help in this.

When the first batch of emissaries[1] arrived in Iraq in March 1942, their main objective was to set up a network for the transport of Polish and German Jews who had found refuge in the neighbouring Soviet Union and Iran. At a later stage, the emissaries turned their attention to forming a para-military youth organization, called Khalutz (the Pioneer Movement) among Iraqi Jews, as part of a policy of selective emigration, mainly of youth, to Palestine. But evidence suggests that the activities of the emissaries began to decline towards the end of the war and came to a standstill by 1945, when most of them decided to return to Palestine. One emissary, Dan Ram, in a letter dated 9 October 1945 to Yigal Allon, then commander of external operations of the Hagana, acknowledged their failure in Iraq and suggested that they return (quoted by Cohen, 1969, p. 159).

Nine months after the violence in Baghdad, Enzo Sereni, the leader of the Zionist underground movement in Iraq, wrote to the Jewish Agency expressing his astonishment at 'the lack of enthusiasm among the Baghdadi Jews for Palestine'. Sereni attributed this to the 'prosperity' brought on by the war, to what he called 'the Jewish talent for forgetting and adapting', and to the attitude of the Iraqi government, which had paid compensation to the victims of the riot. In September 1942 Sereni concluded

> We should not forget that we missed the opportunity for decisive action by not being here immediately after the massacre, and by not trying before the massacre to prepare the right conditions for exploiting this golden opportunity (quoted by Cohen, 1969, p. 156).

---

1. The original group comprised three people: Ezra Kaduri, Shamarya Gotman, and Enzo Sereni, the leader of the movement, who was later killed in Italy.

Another important factor that might have helped to allay the fears of the Iraqi Jews in the post-war period was the rise in the fortunes of the democratic wing of nationalism (at the expense of the pan-Arabists), with its emphasis on social and local issues. This trend continued up to the establishment of Israel in May 1948. Popular resentment was generally on the rise, as a heavy burden fell on the peasants and the lower-income sections of the Iraqi population. Food shortages, poor harvests, and a decline in oil revenues imposed by the British to help pay for the war created a climate of social tension. The price of many basic commodities rose five- to ten-fold, and they became too expensive for the majority of the population, who were able neither to improve their lot nor to find legal means of voicing their grievances.

In the meantime, the key to British policy in the 1940s remained essentially what it had been in the past: 'to achieve our ends by the use of influence rather than direct exercise of authority'.[1] The pro-British indigenous ruling class clung to its oppressive methods in dealing with any social and democratic demands.

It is important to note that at the peak of the strength of the national movement, which actually took control of the streets of Baghdad during the *wathba* or popular uprising of January 1948,[2] the Jews of Iraq felt more secure and closer to their fellow Iraqis. It was, as some Zionist sources acknowledged, 'an era of brotherhood at a time Palestine looked so remote' (see, for instance, Me'ir, 1973, p. 281 and Atlas, 1969, pp. 243–6).

When a Jewish youth, Shaol Tuweq, was killed by police earlier in June 1946, when joining an anti-government demonstration, the newspaper *al-Yaqtha* (which generally reflected the views of the right-wing pan-Arabist Istiqlal Party and which became notorious

---

1. Minute of Sir A. Cadogan, dated 12 January 1944; FO, file number unclear, E 345/37/93.
2. The *wathba* was a major uprising in February 1948 against the signing of the Portsmouth Treaty with the British, which brought down the government of Salih Jabr. This was one of relatively few periods in Iraq when pan-Arabist and democratic wings of the nationalist movement closed ranks to achieve common objectives.

for its anti-Jewish stand just three months later, during the war in Palestine) portrayed Olwan as 'the martyr of the Iraqi people in their fight for freedom' (5 February 1948). During the following two months *al-Yaqtha* also frequently published lists of names of Jewish contributors to the Arab war effort in Palestine (see the issues of 12, 13, 16, and 17 February, as well as 7 and 28 March 1948).

It is therefore difficult to accept the argument put forward by Cohen (1969, p. 15) in his comments on the anti-Jewish violence of 1941 in Baghdad:

> From the 1920s and especially from the 1940s, anti-Jewish propaganda became more influential. Muslim nationalists began to regard Jews as a national Zionist minority and not as a weak religious minority. As Zionists, Jews were considered traitors to Arab ideals.

Cohen's argument does not help, for instance, in understanding the position taken by religious and national leaders in such Arab countries as Lebanon, Tunisia, Algeria, and Morocco, many of whom supported their Jewish countrymen against the anti-Jewish measures taken by the Vichy regime during the second world war (see Abdo and Kasmieh, 1971). It also fails to distinguish between various trends in the Arab national movement. Even if Cohen had in mind only the pan-Arabists within the movement, it is doubtful that they had yet developed any coherent and consistent position that could be considered a clear departure from the traditional view of the Arab Jews as a religious community.

A more plausible interpretation is that with the advance of Zionism in the late 1940s, and particularly after the establishment of Israel, confusion mounted among some sections of the Arab nationalists. This was aggravated by various factors such as the conceptual vagueness of Zionism itself, which was derived from a rather loose definition of a 'Jewish nation' based on the Jewish religion (see, for instance, Woolfson, 1980, p. 112). The attitudes taken, after the establishment of Israel, by the Arab ruling class and by various extremist elements of the Arab national movement (religious or nationalist) also played a role, as we shall see in chapter 3.

Me'ir Basri, reflecting a widely held belief among Iraqi Jews today, sees no grounds for assuming that the emergence of Arab nationalism necessarily had to alter the position of the Jewish populations as a religious community in the Arab countries. 'If Israel had not been established', he said, 'nothing would have happened to the Iraqi Jews. They could have stayed as any other religious minority.'

THREE

Tension Mounts

Under the Iraqi constitution of 1932, Jews had the same civil rights as all other Iraqis. They also had the right to manage their own community affairs and sent four representatives to the Chamber of Deputies.[1] The Chamber was dominated primarily by rich merchants, high-ranking civil servants, tribal chiefs, and religious leaders, a composition that was also reflected in the Jewish section, which generally steered clear of the feuds of mainstream politics and maintained good relations with most successive governments.

Indeed, Iraqi Jews had generally kept out of politics for generations. This passive role may be attributed to their assessment of their position as a weak minority whose economic conditions were nonetheless favourable. Even when the rising Iraqi middle class was able to form social and political societies under the monarchy, the Jewish middle-class intelligentsia seemed generally reluctant to join or to follow suit.

But the second world war, the violence of June 1941, which left the Jewish community with a sense of insecurity, the emergence of the democratic wing as the leading force of the national movement, and later the advance by Zionism eventually had their effects on the Jewish intelligentsia. The passive attitudes of the older generation increasingly came to be questioned. Some saw these attitudes as responsible for alienating the Jewish community from broad sections

---

1. The number was increased to six in 1946.

of the Iraqi people. Some joined political parties, mainly the Iraqi Communist Party (ICP). They saw their future within the mainstream of the Iraqi masses. A 1946 handbill drafted by a Jewish Communist and issued in the name of the Free Jewish Youth, for example, stated:

> Minorities cannot have peace of mind, nor will their social existence be secure until the Iraqi working class attains power. This is what drives the vanguard of the conscious Jewish youth towards the Communists of the toiling masses. (Quoted by Batatu, 2004, p. 651.)

Others, especially young men from less wealthy families, joined the Zionist movement established by emissaries from Palestine. The activities of these emissaries were now aided by the successes of the Zionist movement internationally, primarily the UN resolution of November 1947, which recognized the Zionist demand for the establishment of a Jewish state in part of Palestine, and the proclamation of the state of Israel in May 1948.

Communism and Zionism became the major rival influences among the younger generation of the Jewish community in the late 1940s. Political activism, however, remained largely confined to this younger generation, while the majority of the community remained faithful to its traditional stance of non-involvement.

The Jewish Intelligentsia and the Democratic Movement

In contrast to Egypt, Lebanon, and Palestine, where European Jews played an active role in the foundation of the local Communist parties, in Iraq Jews played no part whatsoever in the birth of the ICP and came into the picture only when Communism had become a significant force in the country. The prominent role of Christians in the early days of the ICP is explained by Batatu (2004) in terms of 'the social disabilities suffered by religious minorities'. But he feels that this was a minor factor in the case of the Jews, who do not appear to have minded much their exclusion from certain political and social roles and in an economic sense were better off than all other communities. Indeed their relative prosperity amidst general distress became a source of danger to them. This factor, and to a much greater extent, the after-effects of the advance of Zionism in Palestine, combined to place their entire position in Iraq in jeopardy. It is therefore, in the first place, to a growing sense of insecurity that has to be attributed the drift of Jewish intellectuals towards Communism in the forties (p. 651).

In early 1946 Iraq witnessed a short period of liberalization as the democratic elements emerged as a major force in post-war politics. Five political parties flourished,[1] but the government soon tightened its control of their activities, while continuing to pay lip service to their value. It was during this period that the Jewish intelligentsia first became politically active. Some joined the left-of-centre National Democratic Party and contributed to its newspaper (see Darwish, 1981). Many others joined the underground ICP, which faced harassment and persecution by the authorities.

According to Batatu (2004), Jews seem not to have been among the members of the politbureau or to have played a significant part in the party leadership until the arrest of the ICP's founder and secretary-general, Yusuf Salman Yusuf (Fahd), in 1947. Their representation in the various Central Committees of the period 1941–47 and at both the 1941 party conference and the 1945 congress was small, absolutely and relatively. Batatu, however, points out that Jews had a major influence in the party's women's organization. The Jewish membership was concentrated largely in the capital, with significant representation in the middle and lower echelons of the greater Baghdad party organization. Because of this concentration, Jews guided the destiny of the party for brief periods after Fahd's arrest (April–August 1947 and December 1948 –February 1949).

---

1. They were: the (mostly) right wing, pan-Arabist Istiqlal Party; the centrist Liberal Party; the left centre National Democratic Party; the left-wing Party of National Unity; and the People's Party.

When the ICP was refused permission to operate during the liberalization of 1946, the Communists managed to secure official authorization for a less controversial platform and set up the Anti-Zionist League (AZL). The idea probably derived from a similar organization set up in Egypt in 1942 by democratic activists among the Egyptian Jewish intelligentsia. Its aims were to 'fight Zionism, oppose Jewish emigration to Palestine, and associate the Jews with the interests of the Egyptian people and the Egyptian national movement' (see, for example, Gunayim, 1969; Nassar, 1980).

The authorization of the AZL on 16 March 1946 was a significant development for both the Communists and the Jewish community. The Communists needed a platform to express their views, while many Jews saw it as an opportunity to reaffirm their identity as Iraqis and to disassociate themselves from the Zionist movement.

The AZL may have been the richest opportunity the Baghdadi Jews had to participate in political life. It succeeded in attracting many intellectuals and bringing them into the limelight. Although the AZL did not consist entirely of Jews, they did form the core membership. Its meetings were well attended and its daily newspaper, *al-Usba*, was widely read. According to one pro-Zionist historian (Atlas, 1969), 'a Zionist meeting in 1946 was attended by three dozen people, while *al-Usba* was printing six thousand copies a day' (p. 247).

The AZL soon established itself as the outspoken representative of the Iraqi Jewish community on the issue of Palestine. Correspondence flowed between the AZL and various local and international bodies. It also managed to make contact with Palestinian nationalists represented by the Supreme Arab Committee, as well as the Executive Committee for Arab Workers in Palestine. Progressive Arab newspapers, especially in Egypt and Lebanon, showed interest in covering the activities of the Iraqi AZL (Yasin, 1972).

The real achievement of the AZL, however, was its contribution to political debates about Zionism at a time when events in Palestine and the attitudes of the pro-British ruling class were creating the greatest confusion among the Iraqi public. In a series of articles in *al-Usba*, signed 'Fahd' and later published in a booklet (*Rasa'il al-Usba*, 1946), the AZL distinguished between Judaism and Zionism, terming the latter a 'colonialist phenomenon'. Other articles (one written by AZL General Secretary Zilkha, 1946, p. 46) explained that 'Jews have no cause other than that of their surrounding societies'. The AZL saw the lack of democracy in Arab countries as providing fertile ground for Zionism; the organization stressed the need to involve the Arab masses, and popular and democratic institutions, in the fight against British colonialism, which was held responsible for the 'founding of the Zionist enterprise in Palestine'.

The AZL foresaw the harm Zionism could do to the Jewish communities in the Arab and Muslim worlds. In a pamphlet issued in November 1945, the founding committee of the AZL[1] warned that, in issuing the Balfour Declaration, Britain and the Zionist movement had sought 'to divert the Arab struggle against the colonialists to one against the Jews and to create a rift that would enable them to go on exploiting the Arab people' (quoted by Yasin, 1972).

When the Anglo-American Commission on Palestine visited Iraq in March 1946, the AZL called on the Arabs to boycott it, on the grounds that it was 'useless, aiming at deceiving the Arabs'. It called on the Arab governments to take the Palestine issue to the UN Security Council, to put an end to the British mandate, and 'to enable the Palestinian people to exercise their right to establish their own democratic state in which all people, without prejudice to their race or religion, can live equally'.[2]

The influence of the AZL extended to some of the wealthier Baghdadi Jews, who had little admiration for Communism but viewed the AZL as a step in the right direction and therefore worth encouraging. Perhaps more significantly, Zionist emissaries saw Communism in general and the AZL in particular as one of the chief obstacles to their activities. As early as 1942, in the favourable

---

1. The founding committee included: Salim Mneche, Nasim Hisquel Yahuda, Masrour Kattan, Ibrahim Naji, Yacoub Masri, Me'ir Yacoub Cohen Ishaq, Moshe Yacoub.
2. *Al Ra'i al-Am* newspaper, no. 1479, 18 March 1946.

climate that followed the British occupation, one of these emissaries wrote from Baghdad: 'One of the major difficulties in attracting the young here is the active role of Communists, which is spreading rapidly' (quoted by Cohen, 1969, p. 173).

As the war came to an end, emissaries complained that their work was in danger of collapse and that the young were deserting the Khalutz (Pioneer Movement) to join the Communists. One of the emissaries who visited Baghdad in 1946 wrote to Palestine asking that his superiors, as a matter of urgency, send someone who could boost the morale of the movement's few remaining activists and encourage them to stay as members (Cohen, 1969, pp. 173–7).

The Soviet Union's abrupt abandonment of its previous policy and its support for the UN resolution of 1947 to partition Palestine severely weakened the Communists' position on the Palestine issue, not only in Iraq but throughout the Arab East. It also brought shock, bewilderment, and disarray in the ranks of the ICP, which had strongly opposed the whole idea of a national home for the Jews. The Jewish members of the party, who had regarded Zionism as 'a danger to the Jews', were perplexed. They themselves had, on 29 May 1946, sent an appeal to the head of the Soviet government, which read in part

> We beseech you, comrade Stalin, to lend support to the cause of Palestine when it comes before the United Nations … The right of its Arab people to independence is unambiguous and their question is unrelated to the plight of the Jewish displaced persons. We are confident that your government, whose principles and foreign policy rest on the right of peoples to self-determination, will side with the Arabs in their tribulation. (Quoted by Batatu, 2004, pp. 597–603.)

The Soviet stand seriously compromised the Communists in the eyes of the masses of people and widened the gulf between them and nationalists of all shades. A year later the gulf narrowed somewhat in the struggle against the Portsmouth Treaty and for democratic rights. But it was skilfully exploited by the ruling class just a few months later, when the military intervention in Palestine was used as an opportunity to crack down on democratic elements in Iraq in May 1948. Jewish democrats were the easiest target, being accused of serving the Zionist cause through their Communist activities.

Three months after the AZL was given permission to function, the authorities banned *al-Usba*. The AZL was dissolved, its leaders arrested and later sentenced to various terms of imprisonment (*Sawt al-Ahali* newspaper, 16 September 1948). To justify their measures, the authorities launched a systematic campaign against the AZL through the official media, accusing it of 'actually serving Zionism and helping to undermine the stability of Iraq' (see al-Rawi, 1977, pp. 123–4). Paradoxically enough, this came at a time when some reports suggested that Zionists were actually threatening the lives of AZL leaders unless they stopped their activities.[1]

An Israeli writer of Iraqi origin (Bar-Moshe, 1975) recalled the argument used by the authorities, paraphrasing one of the judges in the trial of AZL members. This judge alleged that

> the Jews among us could be classified into two categories: the majority, who lack interest in politics, but look to Jerusalem as a religious centre, and the rest, who are engaged in politics, though it is a minority. They do so for the sake of Zionism irrespective of whether they belong to the Communist or other parties … (pp. 198–207).

The evidence, however, suggests that the participation of the Jewish intelligentsia in the nationalist movement of the Arab East during the post-war period did not conform to this view. On the contrary, the integration of at least some Jews in the Iraqi struggle for democratic rights and national independence signalled an end to traditional Jewish abstention from Iraqi political life. In fact, it could well be argued that the totalitarian attitudes of the Arab regimes,

---

1. See the complaint made by AZL chairman Yusuf Zilkha to the judge Khalil Amin. In it he referred to threats to the AZL leaders made by the Zionist radio station in Palestine (see al-Rawi, 1977, p. 134).

themselves still largely under colonial influence, were actually serving the Zionist cause by harassing and persecuting the democratic forces. Indeed, many Zionist historians reported a revival of Zionist activities among the Iraqi Jews immediately after the dissolution of the AZL and the arrest of its activists (see, for example, Cohen, 1969; Me'ir, 1973).

The Israeli Dimension

The proclamation of the state of Israel on 15 May 1948 and the war that followed drastically changed the geopolitics of the entire Middle East. Among the main effects was the realignment of political forces in Iraq. In the two years before 1948, the Iraqi ruling class had faced an increasingly serious crisis. Despite constant harassment, the influence of the democratic forces was growing steadily, amid mounting social distress and popular dissatisfaction. Post-war economic pressures were reflected in a rise in unemployment. A series of strikes hit the nerve centres of the infrastructure: the port of Basra, the railways, and the post office. Some of these strikes led to violence, and in one incident at least sixteen workers were killed by the police (for more details, see Khairi, 1974, p. 146).

The popular struggle of the time centred on demands for democratic rights and on local social and political issues. The regime, which the British had forcibly reinstalled in June 1941, was in retreat. The *wathba* uprising of February 1948, which brought down the government of Saleh Jabr three months before the proclamation of Israeli statehood, illustrated the intensity of the political difficulties of the ruling class and cast doubt on its future stability.[1]

The proclamation of Israel not only transformed the political scene but also shifted the focus away from local issues. The new factor was fully exploited by the ruling classes, not only in Iraq but

---

1. At the time, the British were seriously considering alternatives to the traditional pro-British politicians. See for example: Sir H. Mack to FO, 3 January 1949, FO 371/75128, E 74/1011/93.

in neighbouring Arab countries as well. The Arab armed intervention in Palestine was used to justify the introduction of martial law in the member states of the Arab League, a measure whose main use was to help the Arab governments suppress the growing internal opposition. Wide and vigorous campaigns to crush the democratic elements and wipe out their humble achievements were launched in Egypt, Iraq, Lebanon, Syria, and Jordan (see, for example, *al-Yaqtha* newspaper, 17, 18 and 30 May 1948).

This was perhaps clearest of all in the case of Iraq. The heavy hand of the martial law authorities was felt in many aspects of political life. Meetings were banned, political parties forced to suspend their activities, trade unions dissolved; strict press censorship was imposed. There were many arrests of opposition activists, mostly Communists. Other arrests seem to have been somewhat random. In February 1949, after months of hesitation, the authorities felt able to send four Communist leaders, Fahd among them, to the gallows, and by September of the same year all ICP Central Committee members had been arrested.

This shift in Iraqi internal politics placed the opposition movement in a difficult situation. The ruling class had managed, under the pretext of a national cause, to settle the argument about the need for social and democratic reforms – at least for the time being. After the show of unity and strength during the *wathba*, the national movement divided over many of the issues on which it had previously been united. Under the banner of the national cause, the ruling class had found a new ally: the right-wing nationalists. After the Arab military failure in Palestine, Prime Minister Nuri al-Said formed a coalition with the Istiqlal Party. Both partners saw Zionism as a by-product of Communism,[1] and both seemed more than ready to treat the position of the Iraqi Jews in the context of the hostilities in Palestine.

---

1. The Istiqlal Party joined the government of Nuri al-Said in early 1949 on a coalition programme which paid very little attention to social and political reforms but equated the fight against Communism with the fight against Zionism (see al-Hasani, 1955a, pp. 93–5).

A perusal of the Iraqi press of the period provides vivid illustration of the shift in the attitude of some of the nationalist forces. *Al-Yaqtha*, which reflected the views of the Istiqlal Party, was quick to abandon the tolerant stance it had taken towards the Jews during the *wathba* and began to attack what it called 'the three evils: the Communists, the Zionists, and the Jews'. It criticized 'those who are trying hard to make a false distinction between Zionism and Judaism' (3 May 1948).

In two articles (4 and 23 May 1948), *al-Yaqtha* described Israel as a 'Communist plot against the Arabs' and expressed the view that the Americans were friendlier towards the Arabs than towards the Zionists. A week before Iraqi troops were sent to Palestine, *al-Yaqtha* (7 May 1948) sharply criticized the strike of workers in the oil refineries, accusing the Communists and the Jews of being behind what the newspaper called 'this subversive act aimed at undermining the war effort'. *Al-Yaqtha* concluded

> … They [the workers] want to defy the orders of the high command so as to mislead people and direct their attention away from their prime cause, Palestine … what they want to achieve is worthless. Nothing else is worth as much as a single drop of Arab blood in Palestine.

Al-Yaqtha of 16 May 1948 welcomed the introduction of martial law as a 'necessary measure' to eliminate the 'fifth column' of the enemy inside Iraq. As the Iraqi troops left for Palestine, *al-Yaqtha* entertained its readers with reports of a string of victories from the front. Once the truth about the deficiencies of the Arab armies surfaced, the newspaper turned its wrath against the Iraqi Jews. In his daily column the editor, Sulayman al-Safwani, urged Iraqis to boycott Jewish shops. 'Let us', he wrote on 23 May 1948, 'liberate the people from the economic slavery and domination imposed by the Jewish minority.' When the Zionist forces drove the Arabs across the UN partition lines and advanced to occupy more territory, al-Safwani urged the Arabs to take action against the Jewish communities. 'An eye for an eye, a tooth for a tooth', he wrote on 20 June 1948. 'He who took the first step is to blame.'

In assessing the Iraqi mood at the time, however, it would be wrong to take the attitude of *al-Yaqtha* as representative. Other journals, like *Sawt al-Ahali*, the mouthpiece of the National Democratic Party, *al-Watan*, and other more liberal newspapers did not share the anti-Jewish views of *al-Yaqtha* and in many cases took issue with them. Nevertheless, the fanatical views of *al-Yaqtha* added to the confusion of Iraqi public opinion, aggravated by the attitudes of a basically feeble and short-sighted government.

Repercussions of the Palestine Defeat

The Arab ruling classes of the 1940s were neither willing nor able to stand up to the Zionist threat. Iraq's contribution to the war effort in Palestine (nearly five thousand poorly equipped soldiers) was not an exception. The nature of this contribution had been agreed three weeks before the proclamation of the state of Israel – at a meeting in Amman between the Iraqi regent and King Abdullah of Jordan. Reporting on the results of the meeting, the British ambassador in Baghdad saw the limited Iraqi contribution as a token gesture that the regent was prepared to make in the face of mounting internal pressure.[1]

When the Palestine war ended early in 1949, the Zionists, who had been allotted 57 per cent of the country in the UN partition resolution, occupied 77 per cent. Of the 1,300,000 Arab inhabitants, nearly 900,000 had been displaced and Israel was in possession of entire cities and hundreds of villages that had not been expected to be part of the Jewish state (for more details see Khalidi, 1959, 1971).

---

1. Baghdad to FO, 24 April 1948, telegram no. 444, FO 371/68471, E 5142. For further information on the Iraqi contribution to the war in Palestine, see Mahmoud, Nuri al-Din, 'Muthakkarati an al-Qadia al-Falastiniyah 1948–1949' (My Memoirs on the Palestine Question, 1948–1949), unpublished manuscript (in Arabic).

It was not long before the failure in Palestine seriously undermined the position of the Arab ruling classes, bringing some dramatic changes in the Arab East.[1] To avert complete humiliation in Palestine and to dampen public anger at home, the Iraqi authorities sought the help of the Americans and the British, acting through King Abdullah of Jordan. What was wanted was a face-saving formula that would enable them to recall the Iraqi troops.[2]

The aggressive attitude of the Zionist leadership further undermined the position of the Iraqi ruling class. Already the news of atrocities committed by Zionist forces against the Palestinian Arabs was reaching Iraq, stirring anger and fuelling anti-Jewish sentiments. Waves of Palestinian refugees, the first following the massacre at Deir Yasin on 9 April 1948, arrived in Arab countries in 1948 and 1949 and even until late 1950.[3] Some eight thousand refugees were allowed to stay in Iraq in the summer of 1948. In many cases the Israeli government offered the homes of Arab refugees to newly arrived Jewish immigrants.[4] On 20 July 1948 the Israeli government froze the assets of Palestinian Arabs in all banks and persistently refused to release any funds that might have helped ease the plight of the Palestinian refugees.

These unfortunate developments soon had repercussions on the Iraqi Jews. The Iraqi authorities seemed increasingly willing to accommodate to anti-Jewish demands as a means of diverting the attention of the Iraqi populace from the failure in Palestine and from

---

1. Three military coups took place in Syria during 1949. King Abdullah of Jordan was assassinated in July 1951. This was followed a year later by the military coup in Egypt that put an end to the monarchy and brought Nasser to power.
2. Baghdad to FO, 27 January 1949, telegraph no. 92, FO 371/75133, E 1330.
3. According to the Iraqi Foreign Ministry, hundreds of refugees were thrown out between 28 December 1948 and 13 January 1949, to areas controlled by the Iraqi forces in the Jenin district. They were attacked by Zionist troops after they had started towards the Iraqi front line.
4. In one year (1949) 130,000 Jewish immigrants were settled in Arab houses, principally in Ramla and Lydda, according to Israeli sources (see 'Report on Immigration' based on figures given by the Jewish Agency; Tel-Aviv to FO, 2 February 1950, FO 371/87618 ER 1574/1).

concern with social and political reforms. These attitudes appealed to the government's extremist allies at a time of retreat. Moreover, the persistent persecution of the democratic elements within the national movement made reasoned argument about the position of Iraqi Jews increasingly difficult. The long-standing distinction between Judaism and Zionism was fast becoming blurred, mainly as a result of the events in Palestine and the attitude of the Iraqi authorities.

Although no specific official laws were passed that could be called discriminatory, in practice the position of Iraqi Jews began to deteriorate after May 1948. Some of the measures taken by the Iraqi government could only be interpreted as designed to encourage suspicion against its Jewish subjects. Restrictions were imposed on travel abroad and on disposal of property, for instance. Efforts were made to eliminate Jews from the army, the police, and the public services. According to the Iraqi Foreign Ministry, 796 employees were dismissed from public service between May 1948 and December 1949.[1]

Jews began to feel that they no longer had the economic opportunity they had enjoyed in the past. Jewish banks, for example, were deprived of their licences to deal in foreign exchange. It is impossible to determine whether this was due to mere suspicion or to concrete evidence of attempts to transfer funds abroad illegally.

---

1. The numbers dismissed from various departments were:
    Ministry of Social Affairs, 159
    Ministry of Finance, 51
    Iraq State Railway, 261
    Directorate General of Ports, 109
    Directorate General of Posts and Telegraphs, 38
    Public Works Department, 24
    Ministry of Economics, 11
    Ministry of Interior, 21
    Ministry of Defence, 4
    Ministry of Education, 117
    Department of Civil Aviation, 1
    Total, 796
    (Baghdad to FO, 12 December 1949, FO 371/75183, F 15078).

Jewish merchants found it more difficult to obtain import licences, although the more influential among them did manage to do so. Government contracts were no longer offered to Jewish firms, and some Jewish businesses began to complain of heavier taxation than their Muslim counterparts.[1]

It should be noted that some nationalists viewed the predominant position of the Jews in commerce and the civil service as the result of special privileges granted them under foreign influence (al-Wardi, 1976, p. 42; Kubbah, 1956, pp. 242–3). Such views do not appear to have been expressed publicly, and before the Arab-Israeli war of 1948 they carried no official weight. But now, particularly after the extreme nationalists joined the government of Nuri al-Said, these views began to be reflected in government actions. Mahdi Kubbah, the representative of the Istiqlal Party who held the post of minister of supply in early 1949, recalls in his autobiography (1965, p. 242) how he decided, for instance, to decrease the share of hard currency offered by the government to Jewish importers.

It is doubtful that such measures had much effect on the dominant position of Jews in commerce: businessmen could usually find ways of influencing those in power, as Kubbah himself acknowledged (1965, pp. 245–6), and some of the wealthiest Jewish traders were well connected to people in power (for more details see Batatu, 2004, pp. 311–17).

Many nationalists held the Jews responsible for the economic hardships faced by Iraq in 1948–49. It would be safe to assume that these hardships were aggravated because of the anxieties afflicting the Jewish business community in the climate of uncertainty that prevailed after the war in Palestine. Credit was restricted because of Jewish lack of confidence. Some Muslims claimed that the reluctance of Jews to risk their capital was part of a deliberate policy of injuring the Iraqi economy. The vicious circle of suspicion undoubtedly harmed the economic prospects of Jewish businesses. But it is not

---

1. Baghdad to FO, 21 March 1950, FO 371/82422, EQ 110 3/2.

easy to determine whether the Jewish business community suffered disproportionately to the Iraqi business community as a whole.

Martial law, which was mainly directed against the Communists, was also used by the authorities against the Jews. A number of abuses were reported in the summer of 1948.[1] Such cases seemed to be concentrated in Basra where a Jewish businessman, Shafiq Adas, was hanged publicly in September 1948, for allegedly selling British army scrap to Israel. It is impossible to say whether the charge was true, but what is significant is that although Adas had Muslim partners, none of the others was even punished. His trial was conducted with grotesque publicity, at a time when Arab military failure in Palestine seemed certain.[2]

The Adas episode had important effects on the attitudes of both Jews and non-Jews in Iraq. Adas was one of the country's wealthiest Jews. But he was not closely involved with the Jewish community. His trial and public hanging caused great anxiety among many Jews, for it showed that even a well-connected, fully integrated Jew was not immune. Zionists were able to exploit this feeling of insecurity to argue that the Jews had no future in Iraq. The effect on many non-Jews was to impugn the loyalty of Iraqi Jews, including the most prominent and well-integrated.

---

1. See memorandum by World Jewish Congress, 22 October 1949, on the treatment of the Jewish population in Iraq, submitted to the UN (FO 371/75183).

2. According to British sources, there was a strong element of personal feuding in this case, which brought the resignation of the defence minister, Sadiq al-Bassam, who was held responsible for court-martial abuses against Jews (Baghdad to FO, 'Confidential', 13 January 1949, FO 371/75182, E 770/1571/93). Other reasons behind al-Bassam's resignation cannot be ruled out. He was critical of British policy on Palestine, and this may have weakened his position. In his letter of resignation he accused the British and Americans of plotting against the Arabs. He also complained of 'the consistent intervention' by his colleagues in the cabinet on behalf of the Jews in matters relating to the implementation of martial law. 'Why didn't they raise objections', he asked, 'when thousands of Arabs and Muslims were driven to courts martial in the interests of securing the [Second World] War efforts?' (See al-Hasani, 1955b, pp. 16–17.)

In a memorandum sent by the Iraqi Ministry of Foreign Affairs to the US State Department on 18 November 1948 responding to allegations made by American Zionists that martial law was directed against the Jews, the Ministry reiterated its insistence that the Iraqi authorities were concerned primarily with the Communists, whether they were Jews or not, though it also questioned the reason for 'the increasing number of Communists among the Jews'. The Ministry found it useful to offer some figures to support its argument. It stated that 276 Jews had been convicted under martial law for 'disseminating destructive Communist and Zionist ideologies', compared with 1,188 non-Jews 'most of whom were convicted of impairing security'.[1]

What is perhaps more significant is that in the same memorandum the Ministry drew an analogy between the treatment of Palestinian Arabs in Israel and of Jews in Iraq. Frequent use of this analogy by Arab officials, far from countering Zionist arguments, probably strengthened the Zionist case.[2]

The memorandum also sheds some light on the position taken by the Iraqi authorities. They saw their major fight as against the Communists and their supporters. The abuses against the Jews, which occurred both during and immediately after the war in Palestine, were seen as a side issue. Martial law was considerably relaxed after September 1948. The so-called Third Court in Basra,

---

1. Enclosure no. 1 in Sir H. Mack's dispatch to London, no. 236 (369) 74/49 dated 12 December 1949 (FO 371/75183).

2. It is likely that the Arab officials inherited this analogy from their colonial masters. Reading through the FO documents, one is struck by the fact that British officials often refer to the Zionists or Israelis simply as 'the Jews'. A report sent by the British High Commissioner in Baghdad to London on 13 March 1949, commenting on allegations of maltreatment of Iraqi Jews made by the Board of Deputies of British Jews, said that many of these allegations were exaggerated and some were entirely without foundation. It went on to state, in a manner reminiscent of the structure of Zionist apologetics: 'It is indeed surprising that despite the often extreme provocation of events in Palestine, there has been comparatively little discrimination against the Jews in these countries [the Arab countries].' (Baghdad to FO, 'Confidential', 13 March 1949, FO 371/75187, E 369/5/49.)

set up under martial law, was abolished. When martial law was lifted at the end of 1949, restrictions on the freedom of movement of Jews were eased. American and British reports described the attitudes of the Iraqi authorities during 1949 as 'reasonable and moderate'.[1]

Some Iraqi Jews seem to have seen the government measures as unavoidable and temporary in the light of the hostilities in Palestine. This, at least, is how the head of the community, Chief Rabbi Sassoon Khedouri, viewed them. He found the Iraqi measures less severe, for instance, than those taken by Washington against America's Japanese citizens during the Second World War (see Berger, 1955, p. 34). By the end of the summer of 1949, Iraqi officials and Jewish community leaders alike were trying to minimize the effect of the measures that had been taken earlier, and appeared to be acting in a conciliatory and understanding spirit. In a letter to the Foreign Office dated 27 October 1949, Sir Henry Mack reported that a deputation of leading Iraqi Jews, headed by Khedouri, had been received by Sayid Umar Nadhmi, the acting prime minister, just three days before. According to the letter, the delegation raised four demands: that Jews should not be subjected to special restrictions on travelling abroad; that they ought not to be dismissed from government service simply on grounds of their religion; that they should not continue to be prohibited from buying and selling property; that there should be no discrimination against Jews' obtaining the necessary licences granting access to some professions.

It was reported that Nadhmi had responded as follows. First, the Iraqi government was intending shortly to relax the conditions under which Jews might leave the country. Second, he was personally opposed to dismissal on grounds of religion and did not think that

---

1. Muzahim al-Pachachi, the prime minister at the time, declared in Parliament in January 1949 that he 'would not tolerate any persecution against the Jews' (Baghdad to FO, 'Confidential', 13 January 1949, FO 371/75182, E 770/1571/93). This can be seen as an attempt by al-Pachachi to please some elements within the cabinet, and as an acknowledgement by the authorities of the need to rationalize martial-law practices and to curb the wave of extreme nationalism, which the authorities rode when it suited them in summer 1948. (See also Appendix 2.)

a large number of such dismissals had taken place. Third, the restriction on property dealings would be automatically removed as soon as martial law was lifted. Finally, he added that complaints about discrimination had also been received from other minorities and said that efforts were being made to respond to these complaints by introducing a quota system for entry to the various training colleges.

Commenting on the meeting, Sir Henry Mack later wrote

> In the light of the new situation brought about by the State of Israel, I think it is fair to remark that the Iraqi Government has shown tolerance in their dealings with the Iraqi Jews; and this is borne out by the fact that a Jewish deputation should have been received and answered in the manner I have described, at a time when the Israeli Government is issuing provocative statements.[1]

Zionism in Action

The establishment of Israel had a significant effect on Jewish communities all over the world. The view of the Israeli leadership was that Judaism was best served by ending the 'diaspora'. It claimed the role of representative of world Jewry, a role sometimes disputed by some Jewish communities.[2] As control of world Jewish organizations was gradually secured, the Israeli leadership was able to direct its activities in a manner designed to serve the needs and political interests of the new state. One important new factor was the appreciation by the major powers, especially the United States,

---

1. Baghdad to FO, 27 October 1949, telegram no. 208 (369/36) 49, FO 371/75183.
2. A major dispute erupted soon after the proclamation of Israel when the American Zionists, who were reluctant to migrate to Israel, refused to accept Ben-Gurion's view that immigration was a basic condition for Zionism. See 'Report on 23rd Zionist Congress held in Jerusalem, 14th–30th August 1951', Tel-Aviv to FO, 6 September 1951, FO 371/91751, ER 157210.

that their interests could be well served if Israel played a significant regional role. This gave Israel considerable international leverage.

For ordinary Iraqi Jews, Israel posed the issue of dual allegiance. There was considerable sympathy for the plight of European Jews, for whom Israel offered a home, and probably some pride was felt in the fact that Jews had established a state, thus reinforcing a sense of identity for all Jews. In this respect, their attitude was probably comparable to that of Jews in Britain or the United States. The Iraqi Jews' attitude to Zionism, however, was severely complicated by the conflict it aroused with their other loyalties: to the people among whom they lived, and to their own traditions and culture, which reflected those of the wider Iraqi society. Sympathy for Israel therefore did not extend to commitment to emigration. The correspondent of the *Jewish Chronicle* (30 December 1949) accurately described the dilemma:

> In Iraq, the question of dual allegiance is not an academic one. The founders of modern Iraq built their state on the basis of Arab nationalist theory, according to which Zionism is an aggressive movement which has secured a beachhead in Palestine in order to conquer the whole of the Middle East at a later stage. One cannot, therefore, be a patriotic Iraqi and a sympathizer with Zionism at the same time.

Zionist activities in Iraq were now renewed, but with fresh vigour and a clearer objective: emigration to Israel. These activities were reinforced by the influence of the newly born state and by a well-organized world-wide propaganda machine.

Zionism became a punishable offence in Iraq in July 1948, when the criminal code was amended to characterize Zionism as well as anarchism and Communism as crimes. But there is no evidence that the Iraqi authorities were as concerned with Zionist activities as they were with those of their other internal political opponents. The two major batches of arrests of Zionist activists in October 1949 and June 1951 appear to have been the result of chance discoveries rather than the culmination of concentrated efforts at detection.

Indeed, some sources have suggested that it was an embarrassment to the Iraqi authorities that the arrests were the accidental result of efforts by branches of the police not tainted with Zionist connections (al-Sudani, 1980, pp. 308–09). It has also been suggested that at least some Zionist activities had, through bribery, secured the acquiescence of some senior Iraqi officials (see, for example, Me'ir, 1973).

The Zionists had some success at this stage in recruiting young Jewish members in Iraq. But the extent of their influence was limited by the anxiety that arose in the aftermath of the establishment of Israel. Many Iraqi Jews felt that the present tensions were temporary and would disappear with a peace settlement in Palestine. As long as this view predominated, Zionism could achieve only partial success in Iraq. The critical factor in more lasting and profound success would depend on the extent to which Iraqi Jews came to believe that peace efforts were futile. In that sense, the world-wide Zionist propaganda campaign and Israel's international role were more decisive in determining the fate of the Iraqi Jewish community than the secondary role played by Zionist activists in Iraq itself.

The arrest of Zionist activists in early October 1949 was a by-product of an investigation into Communist activities.[1] According to the director-general of the police, forty-eight Jews were arrested, thirty-three of whom were sentenced to terms of imprisonment ranging from two to five years and fifteen of whom were acquitted.[2] According to Cohen (1969), the October arrests nearly wiped out the Zionist organization in Iraq

> It became necessary to smuggle out about sixty organizers in a short period of time. Only a few organizers remained. If it had not been for the official permission to emigrate a few months later, this crisis would have killed the secret

---

1. A Jewish youth, Said Khalashi, a former member of the Zionist organization TNUA who had later become a Communist, disclosed the names of Zionist activists he knew.
2. Baghdad to FO, 6 January 1950, FO 371/82477, EQ 1571/3.

organization and it would have been necessary to start building it afresh (p. 178).

This supports the view that the influence of Zionism seems to have been the result not of an extensive and powerful organization, but of the successful exploitation of events in a well-orchestrated campaign inside Iraq and abroad. As one of the activists later wrote

> We started building the organization through cells, but it is not easy to build an organization of hundreds or even thousands of members through such cells. We adopted a plan of action based on information about what was taking place in the country. This method was also adopted in other parts of the organization. (Quoted by Cohen, 1969, p. 178.)

The attitudes of the Iraqi authorities, the statements of extremist nationalist elements that confused Judaism with Zionism, the execution of Adas, and the arrests and other restrictions were all exploited by the Zionists to revive memories of the Farhud and to heighten Jewish anxiety and turn it into fear.

An important consequence of the arrests of October 1949 was the unprecedented international Zionist campaign which gave the episode a new dimension. Reports of a 'reign of terror' or of the torture and persecution of thousands of Iraqi Jews supposedly being sent to 'concentration camps' were widely circulated in Europe and the United States (see, for instance, *Jewish Chronicle*, 29 October 1949). This campaign was not only largely unfounded, but was also clearly meant to create prejudice. Some of those involved in the campaign later admitted that accounts of alleged atrocities were sometimes fabricated (see, for example, Me'ir, 1973, p. 402).

Both the British and American governments felt at the time that the Zionist reports had been exaggerated. They made no representations to the Iraqi authorities, as many Zionist organizations had requested. In a confidential telegram sent on 2 November 1949, the British ambassador to Washington explained

… the general view of officials in the State Department is that the [Zionist] agitation has been deliberately worked up for two reasons:

(a) To assist fund-raising in the United States.

(b) To create favourable sentiments in the United Nations Assembly to offset the bad impression caused by the Jewish attitudes to Arab refugees. They suggest that the Israeli Government is fully aware of the Iraqi Jews, but is prepared to be callous towards the community, the bulk of which, as Dr Elath [an Israeli diplomat] admitted, has no wish to transfer its allegiance to Israel.[1]

Whatever its other purposes, the Zionist campaign deepened the suspicion and general unease increasingly felt by the Iraqi Jewish community. Radio Israel began transmitting special programmes to the Iraqi Jews promising their 'salvation'.[2] An Israeli newspaper went further, asking the government to 'declare all Iraqi Jews citizens of Israel, and give them protection'.[3]

The Zionist campaign gave comfort neither to the leadership of the Jewish community nor to the Iraqi authorities. It came when the furor caused by the war in Palestine was beginning to abate and both sides were striving to overcome its aftermath. The Iraqi government found itself in a dilemma. The arrest of Zionists could be used to justify continuation of the restrictions that had been imposed on the Jews. Yet the Zionist campaign was clearly damaging Iraq's international reputation. The government was not used to this kind of international attack, nor was it equipped to counter the Zionist propaganda machine.

The Iraqi reaction is illustrated by a letter sent by the Iraqi Foreign Ministry to the British and American governments on 8 November 1949, following a Zionist demonstration against the Iraqi

1. Washington to FO, telegram no. 5182, 2 November 1949, FO 371/75187.
2. Tel-Aviv to FO, 27 October 1949, FO 371/75197, E 1307/1571/93.
3. *Haboer*, date unknown, see FO 371/751182, E 12899.

consulate in New York.[1] The letter stated that the Iraqi government took a serious view of the demonstrations, because of what it described as the violent repercussions and reaction that might take place in Iraq. The government explained that it had already issued instructions to the press and broadcasting stations to ban any reference to these demonstrations.[2]

Given the helpless position of the Iraqi government and the seriously weakened influence of the Communists, the only force that could have countered Zionist propaganda was the leadership of the Jewish community itself. But this leadership lacked coherence and was only modestly successful in obtaining significant and timely changes in government policy. Commenting on the difficult task facing the community's leadership at the time, Chief Rabbi Sassoon Khedouri recalled

> … the big propaganda guns were already going off in the United States. American dollars were going to save the Iraqi Jews – whether Iraqi Jews needed saving or not. There were daily pogroms in the *New York Times* under datelines which few noticed were from Tel-Aviv … Why didn't someone point out that the solid, responsible leadership of Iraqi Jews believed this to be their country in good times and bad – and were convinced the trouble would pass? (Quoted by Berger, 1955, p. 30.)

---

1. Government of Iraq, Ministry of Foreign Affairs, 8 November 1949.
2. The Iraqi letter (as well as some statements given by Arab officials, mainly at the UN) should be seen as a piece of rhetoric, reflecting the position of an impotent government and designed to gain the sympathy of allies, rather than (as interpreted by Zionists) as a threat to the safety of Iraqi Jews. See, for instance, statements given by the Syrian delegate to the UN, Faris al-Khouri (*New York Times*, 19 February 1947); also by the Egyptian delegate (*Manchester Guardian*, 25 November 1947). Yet the Political Committee of the Arab League produced a resolution on 9 February 1948 in which the member states agreed to take 'a harsh stand against any anti-Jewish acts which could harm the Jews of Arab countries' (see al-Hasani, 1955a, p. 292).

The Zionist campaign of autumn 1949 and the Iraqi reaction seemed to have set the scene for developments to come. The destiny of the Jewish community became increasingly tied to a conflict sought by the Zionists and apparently gradually conceded by the Iraqi authorities. Khedouri's resignation as the head of the community on 11 December 1949 can be considered as an omen, for it was a defeat for the leadership of the community. This leadership did not accurately reflect the social composition of the Iraqi Jews. The committee was dominated by professionals and well-to-do merchants who enjoyed good contacts with leading politicians and officials, so that the predominant view was that of the establishment Jews. Their credibility, however, rested on their ability to win the lifting of restrictions and to achieve real improvements. The leadership seemed to have expected some significant concessions when it met the acting prime minister in October 1949. As the inflamed feelings aroused by the war in Palestine cooled, there was some optimism that a solution to the Israeli-Arab conflict would soon be found. The Iraqi government may have been reacting cautiously to the Zionist campaign to see whether that optimism was justified. In any event, the delegation achieved only modest success. Although some of the promises were fulfilled, attacks on the leadership continued, and dissatisfaction with the chief rabbi was widespread. His successor, Heskail Shemtob, was also well-established and prominent, but the former chief rabbi's resignation was seen as a defeat for his policy and a victory for the Zionists, who instigated attacks on him following the October arrests.

Commenting on Khedouri's resignation, the *Jewish Chronicle* (30 December 1949) acknowledged that the rabbi had the support of most of the influential members of the community. The newspaper wrote:

> Sassoon and those Baghdadi Jews with anything to lose dislike Zionism because it has brought them misery. They know that there were anti-Jewish outbreaks in Baghdad before Zionism, but on the whole, Islamic tolerance has enabled Baghdadi Jews to flourish as a centre of learning and

commerce. They and their kind would like to stay. They are attached to their homes, traditions and their shrines of the prophets, and would not like to leave them in order to begin life once more in an immigrants' camp in Israel, where they believe people are not particularly friendly to oriental Jews.

FOUR

Denaturalization

On 4 March 1950, the Iraqi government of al-Suwaidi secured the passage through the Chamber of Deputies and the Senate of Law 1/1950. This law, introduced as an annex to the Ordinance for the Cancellation of Iraqi Nationality (Law 62/1933), empowered the Council of Ministers 'to deprive any Iraqi who wished, of his own free will and choice, to leave Iraq for good, of his Iraqi nationality'.[1] No measures dealing with financial or other arrangements were announced at the time. The minister of the interior, Saleh Jabr, replying to a question raised in the Chamber, said that the government felt that it was not in the national interest to prevent the emigration of those who wanted to leave the country. He said:

> Those who want to do so for good would do the country harm if they remained. As to the remaining Jewish nationals, the government considers them as Iraqis equal with Muslims and Christians ... the constitution is a guarantee of this.[2]

The new law seemed to relieve the tensions of the previous two years, and was generally welcomed by the Jewish community as a liberal measure. A similar view was taken by al-Suwaidi himself. He was quoted as saying that both Jews and Muslims were pleased with

---

1. See Appendix 1 for the full text of the law.
2. Baghdad to FO, 21 March 1950, FO 371/82478, EQ 1571/17/50.

the law. 'The Jews', he said, 'felt that the departure of malcontents would facilitate good treatment for the remainder.'[1]

The Iraqi government's main justification of the law was the rising rate of illegal Jewish emigration. Under martial law, attempts by Jews to leave the country illegally could be severely punished, offenders being charged, for example, with 'attempting to join the Zionist bands in Palestine'. When martial law was lifted in December 1949, illegal emigrants would be prosecuted only under passport law 65/1932, the offender being liable to a maximum penalty of six months' imprisonment or a fine of 100 Iraqi dinars.[2]

The official concern with illegal emigration was understandable, since government sources estimated that some three thousand Jews left the country in this way before Law 1/1950 was passed. This had caused embarrassment to the authorities. There was criticism by the press and the opposition, as reports that such emigration was facilitated by corruption gained wide credence.[3] Perhaps even more worrying to the Iraqi government was the manipulation by Zionist propaganda of any attempt to stop such emigration. The Iraqi government was already the subject of world-wide attack after death sentences had been pronounced on seven illegal emigrants tried in absentia.[4]

The al-Suwaidi government also saw Law 1/1950 as a way of getting rid of what it called 'the disloyal and subversive elements' among the Jews. In their view, these elements included Communists as well as Zionists. Senior Iraqi officials made no secret of their

---

1. Baghdad to FO, 7 March 1950, FO 371/82478, EQ 1571/8.
2. Baghdad to FO, date unclear, FO 371/82478, EQ 1571/6.
3. Baghdad to FO, 1 April 1950, FO 371/82479, EQ 1571/16.
4. The Iraqi government came under Zionist attack in March 1949, when it sentenced to death seven Jews who had crossed the border while martial law was still in force. The Zionists ignored the fact that those men were already outside Iraq, and a world-wide campaign was launched as if the seven men were going to die. The United Nations and all Western countries were asked to intervene, while demonstrations were organized in New York demanding the abandonment of armistice negotiations 'unless Iraq would agree to spare the men'. Washington to FO, 22 March 1959, FO 371/75182, EQ 1571/93.

annoyance at the presence of Jews among the Communists.[1] This view may have been influenced by reports that authorities in neighbouring Iran were encouraging about three thousand Jewish sympathizers of Tudeh (the Iranian Communist Party) to leave the country.[2]

Many studies, however, while not rejecting all the official Iraqi justifications out of hand, see the law as the result of continuous pressure on Iraq from the British, American, and Israeli governments.[3] Some studies go further, regarding Law 1/1950 as the culmination of secret negotiations involving these parties together with the al-Suwaidi government.[4] Neither sort of study produces any real evidence to support these views. The credence sometimes accorded these claims seems to arise from the fact that the long-term consequences of the new law proved to be neither benevolent nor liberal: the developments that followed the passing of the law led eventually to the evacuation of almost the entire Jewish community to Israel between summer 1950 and summer 1951. The law itself seems not to have been unrelated to a variety of 'transfer schemes' calling for the resettlement of Arab refugees in Iraq and the mass emigration of Iraqi Jews to Israel. The transfer schemes and the denaturalization law formed the prelude to the Iraqi Jewish exodus.

---

1. In a memorandum dated 18 November 1948, sent to the State Department of the United States from the Iraqi Ministry of Foreign Affairs. The Ministry offered its own explanation for the increasing number of Communists among Iraqi Jews: 'Zionism', the memorandum reads, 'had exploited Iraqi Jews for its own ends and interests and induced them to participate in destructive Communist activities.' FO 371/75182, EQ 1571/93.

2. Tehran to FO, 20 May 1950, FO 371/82481 no. 1471/15/50.

3. See, e.g., Darwish (1981, p. 69), who refers to British involvement, while Cohen (1969, p. 195) suggests that the Americans might have exerted some pressure.

4. Abu Mazin (1976, p. 83), without giving any source, states that the denaturalization law was discussed and agreed upon by Nuri al-Said, Ben-Gurion, and a British official, in a secret meeting held in Vienna in 1949.

The Transfer Schemes

The idea of initiating population transfers, expelling Arabs from Palestine and bringing in Jews (including those communities in Arab countries), was not a new one in Zionist thinking. The 'revisionist' wing of the Zionist movement was probably more open about it at an early stage, but the idea had also been entertained by the mainstream 'socialist' leadership of the movement.

Joseph Weitz, a dedicated revisionist Zionist and administrator responsible for Jewish colonization, wrote in his diary, published in 1940:

> Between ourselves it must be clear that there is no room for both people together in this country [Palestine] ... There is no other way than to transfer the Arabs from here to the neighbouring countries; to transfer all of them, not one village, not one tribe, should be left ... only after this transfer will the country be able to absorb the millions of our own brethren. There is no other way out. (Quoted by *Davar*, 29 September 1967.)

The case for such transfers was also pressed by the official leadership of the Zionist movement during the Congress of the World Council of Poale Zion (Union of Zionist Workers), held in Zurich in 1937. Speaking at the Congress, A. Cizling, one of the leaders of Mapam (a socialist Zionist party), said

> I do not contest our moral right to advocate an exchange of populations ... The possibility is more real and more sensible, to operate an actual exchange of populations between a united Land of Israel, some time in the future, and Iraq and other Arab countries, by way of the transfer of their Jews to Eretz Israel. And if this vision is also far remote, at least it coincides with interests that are quite compatible with it. (Quoted by Woolfson, 1980, p. 122.)

Ben-Gurion, discussing this proposal at the Congress, did not rule out the possibility of implementing the transfer by coercion.

The transfer idea received special attention on the international scene in 1936, when the Peel Commission on Palestine recommended an exchange of land and population. After successful Zionist lobbying, the National Executive of the British Labour Party officially adopted the idea at its annual conference of 1944 (Hirst, 1977, p. 131).

In the case of Iraq, there is some evidence to suggest that the exchange of Iraqi Jews for Palestinian Arabs may have been put forward on various occasions in the twenties and early thirties, although it is not clear whether these proposals had the official backing of the mandatory authority or were simply personal views expressed by some British and international Zionist figures.[1]

American Zionists, characteristically, were somewhat reticent about a proposal from ex-president Hoover, who called for 'engineering' the transfer of the Palestinians to Iraq. The American Zionist Emergency Council of 1945 declared:

> The Zionist movement has never advocated the transfer of Palestine's Arab population … Nevertheless, when all long-accepted remedies seem to fail it is time to consider new approaches. The Hoover Plan … represents an important new approach in the realization of which Zionists would be happy to co-operate with the great powers and the Arabs. (Quoted by Hirst, 1977, p. 131.)

With the establishment of Israel, the transfer project seemed more realistic. Part of the scheme had already been achieved with the

---

1. In an interview with the author, H. Kojman, an Iraqi Jewish writer now living in London, recalled hearing accounts of King Faysal of Iraq foreseeing the possible transfer of Iraqi Jews to Palestine, in a meeting with Jewish notables in al-Amara in the early 1920s. In another account, the Iraqi consulate in Jeddah (Saudi Arabia) sent a letter to Baghdad in early January 1933 asking about 'a rumour that the Iraqi government had agreed to a proposal to exchange Iraqi Jews for Palestinian Arabs' (see al-Sudani, 1980, pp. 191–2).

expulsion of the Palestinian Arabs. Of more than one million at the beginning of the Palestine war, only one hundred and fifty thousand Arabs remained in territories occupied by Israel by 1949. The Israelis repeatedly refused repatriation or payment of compensation to the Palestinians. In one of many Arab memoranda presented to the Palestine Conciliation Commission, set up by the UN at the time, the Iraqi government complained about Israeli intransigence: 'Each time', the statement read, 'the Economic Advisers [of the Commission] were about to gain acceptance of a proposal, the Israelis created difficulties and submitted fresh conditions.'[1]

Given this intransigence, the British, at least as early as summer 1949, proposed various schemes to resettle the Palestinian refugees in Arab countries, mainly Iraq. In two separate reports prepared by the British Embassy in Baghdad and sent to London on 14 July 1949, it was estimated that within ten years, one hundred thousand Palestinian refugees could be resettled in Iraq.[2] The proposal, according to the two reports, would require the implementation of various development plans in rural regions, mainly in the mid-Euphrates area.

It was clear that the British ideas were prompted by the hardening attitudes of the Israelis, which the British accepted as irreversible. As one of the reports acknowledged in its introduction: 'There now seems little hope of getting the Israelis either to modify their existing territorial boundaries … or to agree to take back refugees in circumstances in which they will stay.'[3]

What might also have encouraged the British to float the resettlement idea is that they, together with the Americans, were involved in efforts to set up a Western-dominated regional-security arrangement in the Middle East. In summer 1949 President Truman

---

1. Memorandum by the Ministry of Foreign Affairs dated 16 April 1951, FO 371/ 87618, ER 1571/1.
2. Baghdad to FO, 14 July 1949, FO 371/75152, no. 510, 52/49.
3. Ibid.

called for 'constructive cooperation' between Middle Eastern nations affected by the recent hostilities.[1]

The British, who were steadily losing influence in favour of the Americans, were eager to maintain some foothold in the Middle East to protect their interests. And they, perhaps more than the newcomer Americans, were aware of the need for a solution in Palestine if the proposed security scheme was to have any reality.

It soon became clear, however, that British ideas on resettlement were ill thought out. The Iraqis and the Palestinians were hardly enthusiastic. Moreover, the resettlement was also dependent on sweeping development and irrigation projects, for which Washington was expected to pay. When the US government failed to show any willingness to do this, the credibility of the scheme was seriously undermined.[2]

In autumn 1949 the resettlement scheme was given a new dimension as large numbers of Jews from Arab countries began emigrating to Israel. This movement of population was the culmination of Zionist efforts initiated immediately after the proclamation of the Jewish state. They were bolstered by the stance of London and Washington, who saw such population shifts as a new element that might be used in settling the Palestinian question. This could be done, Foreign Office documents suggested, by formalizing de facto transfers through a mutual understanding between Arab states (mainly Iraq) and Israel. Recent evidence suggests that such a proposal was under active, behind-the-scenes consideration a few months before Law 1/1950 was issued.

Foreign Office documents reveal that in autumn 1949 the British government was considering a proposal to exchange one hundred thousand Palestinian refugees for an equal number of Iraqi Jews. The FO wrote to the British legations in the Middle East on 5 September soliciting their views of such a proposal. After alluding

---

1. Washington to FO, telegram no. 4073, 27 August 1949, E 10439/1821/31.
2. FO to Baghdad, 30 May 1950, FO 371/824361, telegram no. 359.

to what it called Nuri al-Said's 'threat' to expel the Iraqi Jews, the letter went on:

> If this threat could be transmuted into an arrangement whereby Iraqi Jews moved into Israel, received compensation for their property from the Israeli government, while the Arab refugees were installed with the property in Iraq, there would seem to be something to commend it. The economic disadvantages to Iraq caused by the removal of a useful element in its population could to some extent be reduced by bringing in Palestinian Arab townsmen in their place. Iraq would be relieved of a minority whose position is always liable to add to the difficulties of maintaining public order in time of tension. For its part, the Israeli government would find it hard to resist an opportunity of bringing a substantial number of Jews to Israel.[1]

There is reason to believe that the Foreign Office's mention of Nuri al-Said's 'threat' was somewhat fanciful and ironically gave it more substance than it actually had. According to a telegram sent to London by Sir Henry Mack, the British ambassador in Baghdad, on 24 February 1949, al-Said had made the comment privately in January 1949, and it was not to be taken seriously. Mack explained that al-Said 'had no intention of proceeding with his threat', but rather regarded it as 'a measure of substantive retaliation if the Jews are not reasonable over Arab refugees'.[2]

It is worth noting that at the time the FO felt that it should advise al-Said against expelling Jews from Iraq. Mack's explanation of 24 February was actually a reply to a telegram, dated 19 February 1949, that the FO had sent to Baghdad. In it the FO suggested some arguments Mack could use in his talk with al-Said.

---

1. FO to Baghdad, 5 September 1949, FO 371/75152, E 9114/1105/93.
2. Baghdad to FO, 24 February 1949, FO 371/75182, E 2334/1571/93. It is also likely that al-Said was piqued by the Zionist reaction to the death sentence issued in absentia against seven illegal immigrants (see note 6 above).

The main argument is that the expulsion of Jews from Iraq would provide an excuse for refusing to pay compensation for the property of Arab refugees. It would be fatal to do anything which might weaken the Arab case in this connection, and I trust Nuri can be persuaded to hold his hand.[1]

There is some evidence in FO documents, however, that the British transfer proposal was not new and that London was in fact echoing similar views expressed by some prominent Zionist figures in the United States and Britain at least several months before al-Said was reported to have made his comment about expelling Jews. Among those figures was Viscount H. Samuel, the first high commissioner in Palestine.[2]

It is puzzling that al-Said's 'threat' appears to have been ignored for six months. No mention of it is found in FO papers between February 1949 and 5 September 1949, the date of the letter about the transfer scheme. While there is no direct evidence that the FO sought the views of the Iraqi authorities on the proposed scheme, it was the subject of some newspaper comments (for example, in *al-Zaman*, 24 October 1949). The Iraqi position, at least officially and as presented in FO documents, had always been to oppose any such

---

1. FO to Baghdad, 5 June 1950, FO 371/82239, EE 1828/22.
2. After the Iraqi government decided in March 1951 to freeze the assets of all Jews who relinquished their nationality, the British consulate general in Jerusalem wrote to the FO: 'It may be of at least academic interest if I now place on record a remark made to me by Viscount Samuel when he was in Palestine in 1949. He called, and had tea with my wife and I on his way back to Israel, after having lunched with King Abdullah at Shuneh. While discussing the seizure of Arab property by the Jews, Lord Samuel said that the obvious way to settle this question was for the Iraqis to turn out their Jews and seize their property, and set this off against the Arab property which the Jews had seized in Palestine.' (Jerusalem to FO, 24 March 1951, FO 371/91690, eq 1571/45.) On the other hand, during the debate in the Iraqi Senate on the denaturalization law 1/1950, Muzahim al-Pachachi was one of the few who spoke in favour of the transfer scheme. Even then, he referred to the proposal 'as was put originally by an American Zionist writer' (see: Baghdad to FO, 21 March 1950, FO 371/82478, EQ 1571/17/50).

scheme, as is clearly illustrated in a letter sent by Sir Henry Mack to London on 5 June 1950, three months after Law 1/1950 was passed.

> My views on this suggestion are as follows. The Iraqi government would probably be willing to accept individual refugees to fill positions which have been or will be vacated by Iraqi Jews ... ex-Palestinian railway officials, for example. I do, however, consider that an exchange of Iraqi Jews for Palestinian refugees on a large scale is neither practicable nor desirable. The Iraqi government still adheres to the proposition that the Arab refugees should return to their homes or be compensated by Israel. It seems therefore very unlikely that they would agree to a mass exchange on a head-for-head basis. If they did agree it is likely that the Jews who are leaving of their own free will would be compromised, and the Iraqi government might use the Jewish property left in Iraq for resettlement of Arab refugee immigrants. Any large-scale immigration would be handled by the Iraqi government with a degree of incompetence which would certainly cause suffering to those involved. Moreover, I am informed that most Palestinian refugees would not wish to come to Iraq while any possibility remains of their being settled nearer to their old home.[1]

What was new in the transfer scheme was that the FO now seemed to have abandoned the idea of settling the Palestinian refugees in the rural areas of Iraq, as had been suggested in summer 1949. The idea now seemed to be simply to settle them in vacated Jewish property in the towns and urban centres. It also seems clear that the FO was now proposing that Israel, which had taken over the properties of the Palestinians, be asked to pay compensation for the properties of Iraqi Jews instead of the Iraqi government.[2]

---

1. Baghdad to FO, 5 June 1950e, FO 371/82239, EE 1828/22.
2. FO to Baghdad, 5 September 1949, FO 371/75125, E 9114/1105/93.

The Foreign Office felt that any anticipated economic and social difficulties could be overcome if the exchange came about as the result of an arrangement between the parties involved – Iraq and Israel – under the supervision of an international commission.[1]

Some British officials thought that the transfer might serve British interests, noting with concern that the Jewish communities in countries under British influence in the region (like Iraq) might otherwise support an Israeli policy of 'economic integration' in the Middle East.[2] Although this view was not pressed strongly in the debate, the anxiety some British officials expressed about the prospects for their government's influence is of some interest, as an indication of how at least some of these officials viewed the regional role that Israel might play in the future.

It is not clear whether the United States government shared the British enthusiasm for achieving a consensus on the transfer scheme. What is certain, though, is that Washington was well aware of the British ideas. Copies of the relevant correspondence were regularly conveyed to the State Department. For their part, American officials were trying to assess the extent of support among Iraqi Jews for the idea of emigration to Israel, at least a year before the denaturalization law was issued. A comprehensive report on the question of emigration of the Iraqi Jewish community was prepared by the American Embassy in Baghdad (dated 8 March 1949) and sent to Washington in a telegram classified 'secret'.[3] The report was written by the Embassy in reply to inquiries raised by the State Department in a telegram dated 7 February 1949. The questions were designed to probe the attitudes of the Iraqi government and the Iraqi Jewish community concerning the possibility of Jewish emigration and its economic effects.

This report seems to mark the beginning of American interest in the fate of the Iraqi Jews. When it appeared that London was failing to bring about a consensus on the transfer scheme, Washington was

---

1. Ibid.
2. See Appendix 3.
3. See Appendix 2.

ready to step in; American influence could be felt more clearly during the crucial months that followed promulgation of the denaturalization law.

The Issue of Jewish Property

The transfer scheme faced two major obstacles. One was the view of most British legations in the Middle East that its probable social and political consequences would benefit neither Iraq nor the Jewish community and that the scheme would not reduce tensions in the region. More serious, however, was the failure to secure the required consensus. Although it is not clear whether the Iraqi authorities were ever officially approached, the Israelis had firm positions on the compensation issue. The Foreign Office held that the Israeli government should assume responsibility for the problem of the Palestinian refugees and pay its share of attempts to resettle them. The Israeli government, on the other hand, was in no mood for compromise. Having seized Arab property, it would not agree to pay compensation, nor was it prepared to accept the British suggestion that Israel compensate the Iraqi Jews for their properties in the event of mass emigration.

Israeli officials seemed to be particularly concerned with the property of Iraqi Jews, who were known for their wealth. In fact, this had been an issue of some concern to the Israeli leadership at an early stage. In a special report prepared by Mossad (the Israeli Intelligence Service) in January 1948, four months before the proclamation of the state of Israel, one Zionist activist in Iraq recalled that it had been proposed to set up a special unit to help in transferring Jewish property and funds from Iraq to Palestine, 'so that the Iraqi Jews would not fall into the clutches of brokers, middlemen, and crooks when the time comes' (Me'ir, 1973, p. 370).

The compensation issue soon became a major preoccupation of the British and Israelis alike. Moshe Sharett, then Israeli foreign minister, put the Israeli view explicitly when the British were still trying to secure approval for the transfer scheme. 'Israel', he said, 'could not in any circumstances agree to receive the Iraqi Jews as penniless displaced persons.'[1]

By the end of 1949, the transfer scheme seems to have been abandoned. It may not have been completely buried, in that the British and Israelis might well have been prepared to revive it under particular circumstances. The conclusion drawn by the FO on 11 November 1949, at the end of the debate, stated:

> Nothing should be done to discourage an amicable arrangement between Iraq and Israel leading to the exchange of Arab refugees for Iraqi Jews. We should not, however, press either the Iraqis or Israelis to initiate action, and if questioned should say that this matter should be left to the governments concerned.[2]

The Israeli government welcomed Law 1/1950, but made manifest an immediate concern for the fate of Jewish property in Iraq. This was in sharp contrast to its attitude to the Yemeni Jews. There have been suggestions that Israel offered the Imam (Yemen's ruler) financial inducements to allow Jews to leave the country. These have for the most part been denied by the American Joint Distribution Committee (AJDC), but it is beyond dispute that all the immovable property of the departing Yemeni Jews was confiscated without compensation. They were allowed to bring with them the tools of their trade and their scrolls (*The Times*, 12 April 1950), arrangements which suggest that some measure of agreement had been reached between Zionist officials and the Imam.

In the case of Iraq there is no evidence that any such agreement existed between the parties concerned regarding either the transfer scheme or compensation at the time when the denaturalization law was passed. There is no evidence directly corroborating the theory that a conspiracy had been hatched in advance.

---

1. Tel-Aviv to FO, 18 October 1949, FO 371/75182, EE 12603.
2. See Appendix 3.

There is ample evidence to support a version of the pressure theory. At the time of the mounting Zionist campaign, the British and American governments were pressing the Iraqi government to open the door for Jewish emigration. It seems, however, that London saw no need for a special law. Any law that was passed, however, would in the British view have to be carefully drafted to avoid charges of anti-Semitism and would also have to be coupled with the lifting of restrictions on those Jews who remained in Iraq.

According to FO documents, both London and Washington were aware of the Iraqi government's intentions before Law 1/1950 was passed. In a dispatch to London, classified 'confidential' and dated 7 March 1950, Humphrey Trevelyan wrote that al-Suwaidi had informed him on 25 February that the cabinet was drafting a law that would allow Jews to leave. Trevelyan listed five points he intended to make to al-Suwaidi about how the denaturalization bill should be drafted. The meeting between al-Suwaidi and Trevelyan at which these points were to have been discussed was scheduled for 2 March. It did not, however, take place.[1]

The conspiracy theory seeks to draw support from the massive scale of Jewish emigration following Law 1/1950. But there is no evidence to suggest that the Iraqi government could have foreseen the developments that led to the exodus. Al-Suwaidi expected that no more than seven thousand Jews might leave the country under the new law, while Saleh Jabr, the interior minister, put the figure at between eight and ten thousand.[2] This assessment by senior Iraqi officials was confirmed by other sources. More important, to my knowledge no sources have suggested that the Iraqi government disbelieved its own estimate or wanted the actual number of emigrants to be higher. Me'ir Basri argues that the official estimates were influenced by the government's desire to keep 'the most loyal elements' among the Iraqi Jews in the country.[3]

---

1. See Appendix 4.
2. Ibid.
3. Interview with the author, London, 6 June 1981.

The pressure theory receives support from Basri, who stated that the Iraqi government genuinely believed that Law 1/1950 would undercut the strength of Zionist propaganda and that it would be favourably received by everyone – the Israelis, the British, the Americans, and the Jewish community itself.[1]

When the Iraqi government issued the denaturalization law, no restrictions were imposed on the property of those who wanted to leave. Despite calls in the parliament to do so, the Iraqi authorities were reluctant to freeze Jewish property in retaliation for the freezing of Arab property and funds in Palestine.[2] More significantly, government reluctance to seize Jewish property came against British advice. According to Trevelyan's letter of 7 March 1950, the British were then urging the Iraqi government to 'study the action taken by the Israeli government in respect to the property left behind by the Arab refugees'.[3]

It was a year before the Nuri al-Said government issued Law 5/1951 and Regulation 3/1951 to freeze the assets of Jews who applied to relinquish their Iraqi nationality.[4] The new law was issued on 8 March 1951, upon the expiry of the denaturalization law. Israel's immediate reaction was to announce through its foreign minister on 10 March that it had decided to charge the value of Jewish property frozen in Iraq against the amount of compensation it might undertake to pay to the Palestinian refugees.[5] Sharret also accused the Iraqi government of hiding its intention to freeze the property until the expiry date for Law 1/1950 and demanded that

---

1. Ibid.
2. Fayiq al-Samarrai and Yusuf al-Mawla, among others, called for such retaliation. See: Proceedings of the Chamber of Deputies, Meeting no. 10, dated 2 March 1950, pp. 142–53.
3. See Appendix 4.
4. See the text of the law (Appendix 5a), of Regulation No. 3 of 1951 (Appendix 5b), and of Supplement Law No. 12, 1951 (Appendix 5c).
5. Speech by M. Sharret, the Israeli Foreign Minister, in the Knesset, 19 March 1951 (Tel-Aviv to FO, 21 March 1951, FO 371/91690, FQ 1571/30).

Iraq 'regularize the liquidation and transfer of the Jewish frozen property'.[1]

The fact that Law 1/1950 was later extended does not invalidate Israel's accusations. There are strong hints that al-Suwaidi's government was aware of British advice to freeze the property but 'preferred to deal with the question gradually'. Trevelyan went on to explain:

> They [the Iraqis] had therefore dealt with the departure of Jews as an amendment to the nationality law, and had decided not to define, at this stage, the amount of money which Jews who wished to leave were to be allowed to take with them.[2]

The reason for the Iraqi government's tactics can only be guessed at. The government was unclear at this stage about how many Jews would leave. It is also possible that the Iraqis still hoped that a settlement of the Arab refugee problem could be reached. At any rate, their official position regarding the Palestinian refugees was clearly stated (see Mack's letter of June 1950).

What is certain is that a considerable amount of Jewish capital was transferred out of Iraq illegally. This could have alerted the Iraqi authorities. It is impossible to give a precise estimate of the amount involved. In justifying Law 5/1951, the deputy governor of the National Bank estimated that capital transferred as of March 1951 (by which time some forty thousand Jews had left Iraq) was in excess of 10 million dinars.[3] This figure did not include the amount of money permitted each Jew leaving the country (50 dinars).

Israeli intransigence on the Palestinian refugees made it difficult to accuse Iraq of maltreating its Jewish citizens; such, at least, was how the British and the American governments saw the situation. Neither expressed any surprise at the Iraqi decision to freeze the property of those Jews who relinquished their nationality. A few

---

1. Ibid.
2. See Appendix 4.
3. Baghdad to FO, 7 March 1951, FO 371/91690, EQ 1572/27.

days before Law 5/1951 who passed, when the Israeli government demanded that the Iraqi Jews should be allowed to leave with 250 instead of 50 dinars each, the State Department apparently felt that there was little point in making an approach to Baghdad on behalf of the Israelis. The British reacted similarly, pointing out that the Israeli proposition would allow an additional 14 million dinars to be taken out of Iraq, an amount equal to more than half the country's budget.[1]

When Law 5/1951 was issued, the Americans and the British again felt that there were no grounds for representation to the Iraqi government. In a letter to the British Embassy in Washington, dated 27 March 1951, the Foreign Office commented: 'We see no likelihood of getting the Iraqis to rescind the law freezing assets, since the Israelis themselves are by no means blameless in this respect.'[2]

Winners and Losers

The debate of 1949 about the proposed transfer scheme produced some intriguing arguments as to who would gain and who would lose as a result of the transfer. One of the main questions raised was whether Iraq would benefit from the emigration of its Jewish community. Another issue – which was not, however, pressed strongly – was whether the mass exodus of Iraqi Jews would harm Israel, given the economic difficulties the country faced in the years immediately after its establishment.

The assessment of the British Embassy was that the Iraqi economy would suffer, especially in the short run, from Jewish emigration. The Americans generally agreed. In its report of March 1949 on 'the Jewish community in Iraq' the American Embassy made a number of observations. First, some 75 per cent of Iraq's import trade was

---

1. Ibid.
2. FO to Washington, 27 March 1951, FO 371/91690, EQ 1371/42.

conducted by Jewish firms. Their role in export trade was probably much less, since the major proportion of this trade (mainly in agricultural products) was in Muslim and foreign hands. Second, the internal distribution of imported goods would be severely disrupted, since a high proportion (estimated at 50 per cent) of importers, wholesalers, and shopkeepers dealing in imported goods were Jews. Third, the small business sector would find it difficult to finance its trade, since a high percentage of internal trade was conducted with the help of *sarrafs* who supplied working capital for small businesses, shopkeepers, and dealers in agricultural products. Most of the *sarrafs* were Jews. Fourth, a drop in real-estate and land values could be expected in the Baghdad area, where a high proportion of the more modern dwellings and business installations were owned by Jews. Finally, before the outbreak of hostilities in Palestine many Muslims considered Jews to be ideally suited for clerical work, and their presence was considered indispensable for the smooth functioning of operations. Clerical staffs in banks, commercial organizations, public utilities, and oil companies were drawn largely from Jewish ranks, and many of these institutions would feel the effect of the Jewish departure.[1]

Because of these likely economic effects, the American report dismissed the possibility that any Iraqi government would permit the mass emigration of the Jewish community.

By contrast, many American and British officials agreed that the emigration of the Iraqi Jews would satisfy Israeli economic and security demands for manpower. The British consulate in Jerusalem, for instance, wrote that the expulsion of Iraqi Jews '… would be welcomed by the Jews here [Israel] who would thus obtain people prepared to work hard for low wages, and the Jews would insist on Iraqis taking displaced Arabs in return'.[2]

Some British officials, however, doubted that the Iraqi Jews, most of them city-dwellers in minor clerical positions, would be of much value to Israel as a source of cheap labour. They also

---

1. See Appendix 2.
2. Jerusalem to FO, 14 February 1949, FO 371/75182, 024566.

questioned the capacity of the Israeli economy to absorb large numbers of Iraqi immigrants. Such views were expressed by the British ambassador in Tel-Aviv, Sir Knox Helm. In a dispatch to London dated 14 October 1949, he wrote

> ... if I were the all-powerful ruler of the Arabs, and wanted to do Israel ill, I should allow no Arab to return here and try to get every Arab out. If, at the same time, I could induce Jews who would add to Israel's economic burden to return here, I should try to do so.[1]

It is not clear whether this view had supporters in the Foreign Office, nor whether it was genuinely felt or was simply meant to influence the Iraqi authorities at a time when the British were interested in selling the transfer scheme to the parties concerned. Later, when Nuri al-Said was trying to speed the departure of Jews who had already relinquished their nationality, some reports suggested that he thought the emigration would do economic harm to Israel.[2] Foreign Office documents suggest other possible reasons for al-Said's concern to speed the departures, as we shall see in chapter 5.

Israel did in fact face economic and financial difficulties in the early 1950s, when four major waves of immigration came in from Yemen, North Africa, Eastern Europe, and Iraq. Israel survived this difficult period with financial aid from the United States. Nevertheless, judging by Israeli statistics on age composition, family structure, and rate of participation in the labour force, it does not seem that Iraqi immigrants were any less attractive than those from Eastern Europe or other oriental communities.

Israeli figures for 1948–52 show that the Iraqi community, like other oriental communities that sent immigrants during the same period, had a high proportion of people under 15. On the other hand, the Iraqi community had a smaller percentage of people 65

---

1. Tel-Aviv to FO, 14 October 1949, FO 371/75152, E 12791.
2. Tel-Aviv to FO, 4 November 1950, FO 371/82984, telegram no. 785.

and over than the Romanian or Polish communities, the largest European groups among the immigrants at that time. (See Table 9.) This made it easier to integrate and absorb the Iraqis into the labour force.

Table 9: Israeli Immigrants by Age, 1948–52 (in %)

Age	From Iraq	From Yemen & Aden	Egyptian Jews, 1937 Census
0–4	13.5	12.3	8.1
5–14	25.5	28.1	21.3
15–29	29.1	26.3	28.7
30–49	17.9	22.1	27.4
50–59	6.8	5.9	8.2
60+	7.2	5.3	6.3

Source: Sicron (1957, Table A 54, p. 42).

The sex composition of the Iraqi Jewish community was almost the same as for the population of Israel as a whole, the percentage of males being 51.3 compared with 50.6 per cent for the whole population. There was a significantly lower percentage of males among the European immigrants, while the North Africans had a high percentage of males (58.9). This was probably because the Iraqi community was evacuated as a whole rather than gradually and selectively, as had happened with the North African Jewish communities. (See Table 10.)

Figures on the marital status of the members of the Iraqi community (for immigrants aged 15 and over) also correspond to those for the total Jewish population during the years 1948–52. It is worth noting, however, that the percentage of young singles – male or female – among the Iraqi community was higher than for the other main immigrant communities. (See Table 11.)

Table 10: Percentage of Males Among Israeli Immigrants, 1948–52

	ASIA AND AFRICA							
	Total	Turkey	Iraq	Iran	Yemen & Aden	Tunisia, Algeria & Morocco	Libya	Other
All ages	51.7	49.8	51.3	48.7	56.9	49.7	52	49.6
0–4	51.7	52.3	52.3	52.5	50.1	51.5	50.7	50.9
5–9	51.9	50.8	52.6	55.5	49.9	51.8	50.9	50.7
10–14	53.4	51.2	53.2	54.3	53.9	56.3	50.5	53.4
15–19	55.9	58.4	52.6	58.2	49	63.2	48.6	56.8
20–24	53.6	51.6	52.1	50.8	43.9	62.9	49.4	56.8
25–29	51.3	54.3	49.3	49.4	44.1	59.6	51	51.2
30–34	49.9	49.8	49.6	51.3	46.1	57.2	46.2	53.9
35–39	48.7	49.3	46.6	48.8	51	52.4	43.4	46.5
40–44	47.2	47.7	49.5	45.9	41.5	45.2	47.2	46.8
45–49	50.4	45.4	53.4	50.7	50	48.3	49.7	49.7
50–54	47	43.7	47.1	49.4	46.2	49.9	47.3	49
55–59	52.1	39.7	55.4	56.9	59.1	36.1	52.8	48.4
60–64	47.2	35.6	48.6	53.3	48.1	58.9	45.6	46.4
65–69	49.6	39.7	50.3	59.8	59.5	55.1	51.2	55.7
70–74	48.1	37.8	50.3	55	50.1	57.8	42.6	47.1
75+	45.4	41.7	49.4	50	51.4	56.9	49	49.5

	EUROPE AND AMERICA								
	Total	Poland	Romania	Bulgaria	Yugoslavia	Hungary	Czecho-slovakia	Germany	Other
All ages	49.6	52.7	45.7	48.8	48.3	53.1	50.8	50.1	52.3
0–4	51.2	51.8	50.4	50.9	51.9	47.4	51.0	52.5	51.2
5–9	49.7	49.4	50.5	50.3	42.1	49.7	49.2	49.0	49.9
10–14	50.6	49.6	50.0	52.0	47.1	55.7	55.2	53.9	51.9
15–19	49.6	49.0	49.1	49.0	48.4	54.8	44.9	51.6	54.0
20–24	45	42.2	42.7	44.9	46.9	51.1	35.7	50.3	45.6
25–29	47.2	46.4	42.9	48.3	40.6	57.8	46.0	47.5	55.5
30–34	49.8	52.0	44.0	46.6	41.3	56.4	51.0	52.6	54.6
35–39	53.7	59.2	45.8	46.6	46.6	58.3	60.6	41.2	54.3
40–44	54		45.9	52.8	51.5	51.0	61.9	50.4	50.3
45–49	50.4	61.0	44.2	50.3	54.5	47.9	61.0	45.9	51.1
50–54	49.4	58.8	46.3	48.7	56.7	47.2	57.4	45.9	48.2
55–59	49.7	57.7	46.9	47.3	54.8	55.0	58.9	48.6	48.3
60–64	45.4	48.4	45.3	45.7	46.0	51.5	55.3	49.0	46.1

EUROPE AND AMERICA

	Total	Poland	Romania	Bulgaria	Yugoslavia	Hungary	Czecho-slovakia	Germany	Other
65–69	45.6	47.6	42.6	50.3	48.0	51.5	42.3	47.8	51.1
70–74	44.7	43.3	42.5	43.8	39.0	46.5	46.7	40.9	49.6
75+	41.7	43.7	40.6	42.9	40.0	46.4	48.0	42.6	43.3

Source: Sicron (1957, table A 54, p. 43).

Table 11: Israeli Immigrants (aged 15 and over) by Marital Status, Sex, Country of Origin, 1948–52 (in %)

	ASIA AND AFRICA							
	Total	Turkey	Iraq	Iran	Yemen & Aden	Tunisia, Algeria & Morocco	Libya	Other
Male:								
Single	43.6	38.6	44.5	42.7	24.1	58.4	35.9	50.6
Married	53.8	58.5	53.3	55.7	69.9	40.2	61.7	46.9
Widower	2.3	2.7	2	1.5	5.7	1.1	2.3	2
Divorced	0.3	0.2	0.2	0.1	0.3	0.3	0.1	0.5
Female:								
Single	25.8	25.2	28.0	24.8	15.6	31.0	25.2	28.6
Married	57.7	56.4	55.9	59.1	62.2	58.0	50.4	56.9
Widow	15.6	17.8	15.5	15.7	21.3	9.1	15.8	12.9
Divorced	0.9	0.6	0.6	0.4	0.9	1.9	0.6	1.6

	EUROPE AND AMERICA								
	Total	Poland	Romania	Bulgaria	Yugoslavia	Hungary	Czecho-slovakia	Germany	Other
Male:									
Single	28	26.5	23.5	21.5	24.8	44.3	29.0	43.8	43.4
Married	67.2	68	71.4	75.7	70.2	52.0	67.5	50.6	52.2
Widower	4.4	5.3	4.6	2.5	4.2	3.3	3.3	3.8	3.6
Divorced	0.4	0.2	0.5	0.3	0.8	0.4	0.2	1.8	0.8
Female:									
Single	18.4	13.7	19.4	14.8	16.4	26	21.3	25.6	25.4
Married	64	73.2	58.5	68.7	60.9	59.8	67.6	56.8	58.4
Widow	16.3	12.6	20.4	15.8	19.5	13.2	10.4	15.2	14.5
Divorced	1.3	0.5	1.7	0.7	3.2	1	0.7	2.4	1.7

Source: Sicron (1957, Table A 54, p. 43).

Although the percentage of dependants and large families was relatively high among the Iraqi immigrants compared with the two main European groups (from Romania and Poland), it was less than that among other main communities from Arab countries: those of Yemen or North Africa. (See Table 12.)

Demographic and short-term economic factors, however, seem to have played a minor role in the formulation of Zionist strategy. Immigration was essential to Israel, for the new-born Jewish state needed labour-power and security.

By the end of 1949, Israel occupied 20 per cent more land than the UN partition resolution had allocated to the Jewish state, while the total population of all the territories occupied by Israel was still less than a third of what it had been before the Palestinian Arab exodus. Moshe Sharret, the Israeli foreign minister, summarized his government's attitude in early 1949 by saying that if 'the position in the Middle East was to be maintained, three million Jews would have to enter Israel by 1952'.[1]

Israel's determination to bring in more immigrants remained undiminished even during the worst of its economic difficulties. During the 1949 general election Mapai (the ruling party), as well as some other parties, declared themselves 'in favour of the early transfer of Jews everywhere to their homeland, with special attention to be paid to Jews in the Arab states'.[2] This view became even more widespread after the Zionist General Council held in Jerusalem in April 1950, when the Israeli government took over most of the responsibilities on matters of immigration and absorption from the Jewish Agency. Ben-Gurion and his associates were pressing for greater immigration and campaigning for the abandonment of the traditional policy of selective immigration for oriental Jews. Among other resolutions, the Council decided: 'The Jewish Agency Executive must endeavour to fit its budget to the task imposed upon it, that no immigration quotas shall apply to the Middle East

---

1. Jerusalem to FO, 26 March 1949, telegram no. 241, FO 371/75261, E 4001.
2. Cairo to FO, 22 September 1949, FO 371/75152, E 11995.

countries', and 'the Jewish Agency must prevent any restrictions on the immigration of Jews who wish to come to Israel'.[1]

Table 12: Israeli Immigrants by Family Status and Country of Origin, 1948–58

Country	Number				Per Cent			
	Total	Un-attached	Head of family	Dependant	Total	Un-attached	Head of family	Dependant
All immigrants	701,890	153,166	165,559	383,163	100	21.9	23.5	54.6
Asia	251190	42420	51212	157,558	100.0	16.9	20.4	62.7
Turkey	34294	9174	7681	17439	100.0	26.8	22.4	50.8
Iraq	122979	30136	23263	79580	100.0	16.4	18.9	64.7
Iran	25733	4072	5270	16391	100.0	15.8	20.5	63.7
Yemen & Aden	47370	4436	10803	32131	100.0	9.4	22.8	67.8
Other	20814	4602	4195	12017	100.0	22.1	20.1	57.8
Africa	94945	25838	17452	51655	100.0	27.2	18.4	54.4
Libya	30689	4790	6390	19509	100.0	15.6	20.8	63.6
Tunisia, Algeria & Morocco	52270	18043	8934	25293	100.0	34.5	17.1	48.4
Other	11986	3005	2128	6853	100.0	25.1	17.7	57.2
Europe & America	355633	84,856	96,874	173,903	100.0	23.8	27.2	49.0
Poland	106121	20784	32182	53155	100.0	19.6	30.3	50.1
Romania	121480	30072	34575	56833	100.0	24.7	28.5	46.8
Bulgaria	36002	4702	10574	20726	100.0	13.1	29.4	57.5
Yugoslavia	7017	1326	2117	3574	100.0	18.9	30.2	50.9
Hungary	13023	5108	2967	4948	100.0	39.2	22.8	38.0
Czecho-slovakia	18438	4815	4957	8606	100.0	26.1	26.9	47.0
Germany	7697	1718	1073	4906	100.0	22.3	13.9	63.8
Other	45855	16331	8429	21095	100.0	35.6	18.4	46.0
Not stated	122	52	21	49				

Source: Sicron (1957, Table A 68, p. 59).

1. 'Report on the Zionist General Council, held in Jerusalem in April 1950', Tel-Aviv to FO, 5 May 1950, FO 371/82618, ER 1574/5.

In fact, as early as summer 1948, while fighting was still going on in Palestine, arrangements were made to bring large numbers of Jews from Arab and Islamic countries, including Iraq (see Hillel, 1977). Representatives of the Jewish Agency, Mossad, and the AJDC were involved, the latter acting as sponsors. Almost the entire Yemeni Jewish community of forty thousand was evacuated to Israel in 1949. During the same period special attention was paid to bringing Jews from North Africa, mainly Morocco. It was only in 1950–51 that the Zionists turned the focus of their attention to Iraq. Once the evacuation of Iraqi Jews had been accomplished, the evacuation of Iranian Jews was placed on the agenda, at the 23rd Zionist Congress in August 1951.[1] Between May 1948 and May 1951 Israel received 310,000 immigrants from Arab and Islamic countries, compared with 276,000 from Europe, America, and the British Commonwealth.[2]

The strategy of the Israeli government was to restructure the oriental communities in accordance with the needs of the Israeli economy, through a process of rehabilitation and training. The original intention was to use funds brought by the wealthier communities – like the Iraqis – to facilitate this absorption. Mossad's report of January 1948 on the Iraqi Jews shows that at that early stage the Zionist leaders were well aware that the Iraqi Jews were a mostly urban community and that efforts and funds would be required if the social and economic structure of this community were to be reshaped to match the needs of Israeli society. The report concluded: 'Effecting the transfer of assets of Iraqi Jews would enable us to use these assets in absorbing the Iraqis, whose emigration to Eretz Israel seems inevitable.'

---

1. According to a British report on the Congress: 'In spite of the wishes of Mr Ben-Gurion to the contrary, the mass plan for tackling the Persian Jews (estimated to number about 80,000) immediately after the end of the Iraq air lift has been dropped for the time being.' The report attributed this to the economic difficulties Israel was having at the time (Tel-Aviv to FO, 11 October 1951, FO 371/91751, ER 1570/14).
2. 'Report on the immigration', Tel-Aviv to FO, 5 July 1951, FO 371/91751, ER 1572/8.

The flow of oriental immigrants – Iraqis among them – between 1948 and 1952 helped Israel to consolidate its claim to all the territories under its military control. This is illustrated by the absorption policy. Behind the chain of kibbutzim strung along the armistice lines, as many as 214 rural settlements (*moshavim*) were set up between 1949 and 1955, with a total population of seventy thousand, 78 per cent of whom were oriental (as of 1960). Most European Jews were settled in very different conditions. The oriental settlers were allocated small plots – about one-tenth of the arable area per capita that had been allocated to European Jewish settlers back in the thirties (Shapiro, 1978).

These territories were also filled with about twenty so-called development towns set up in the more strategic regions, often immediately behind the chain of kibbutzim (Kiryat Shmoneh, Beit-Shan, Ma'alot, Megiddo, Shelerot, Beit-Shemesh, and Kiryat-Gat are some of the 'development towns'). Into these an even larger population, also predominantly oriental, was herded. By 1961, the development towns had a total of 120,000 inhabitants, and two years later the figure had reached 170,000, of which 71 per cent, at the very least, were oriental.[1] The motives for establishing these towns were largely political. Thus an Israeli official source states

> The development towns were set up and populated within the framework of the policy of population dispersal; this policy was designed on the one hand to prevent over-concentration of the population in the coastal region, and on the other hand to populate desolate areas.[2]

---

1. Bank of Israel Annual Report for 1963, Jerusalem, p. 15. According to Shapiro (1978), the figure of 71% refers only to the 'immigrant' population of those towns. A quarter of the inhabitants were in fact Israeli-born, mostly young children of immigrants. Since the birth-rate among oriental Jews is higher than among European Jews, the proportion of oriental Jews among the total population must have been 75% at the very least. The European 25% was largely composed of officials and their families.
2. Ibid.

There was little economic planning, and the development towns in fact proved economically unviable. In 1963, for example, the rate of unemployment in the development towns was 22 per cent (as compared to the national average of 4 per cent), and while their population was only 6 per cent of the country's total, they accounted for as much as 32 per cent of Israel's unemployed.[1]

The economic frailty of the development towns and the *moshavim* suggests that strategic rather than economic considerations were most important in Israel's absorption policy. Furthermore, the emigration of Arab Jews in particular was significant beyond Israeli labour-power strategy. This more than any other emigration fulfilled the basic Zionist concept of population transfer in Palestine.

The effect of the transfer scheme was to let Arab Jews in and to send Palestinian Arabs out of Palestine. This was clearly expressed by M. Sassoon, one of Israel's leading experts on Arab affairs and head of the Middle Eastern Department of the Foreign Ministry. Summing up the prospect of peace with the Arabs in March 1951, he said that 'there would be no real tranquillity in the area until the Jews are out of the Arab states and all Arabs out of Israel.'[2]

The long-term political implications of the Zionist idea of transfer were obvious: to deny the Palestinian Arabs' right to return and their right of self-determination, as recognized by the UN and other international bodies, using the emigration of Arab Jews as a pretext. On many occasions Israeli officials defended the view that a 'spontaneous exchange of population' took place between Arab Jews and Palestinian Arabs, and that the only realistic solution to the problem of the Palestinians was to resettle them in the neighbouring Arab states.[3]

This view, based on sectarian divisions, did not facilitate the integration of the Zionist state, nor did it help to reduce national fanaticism and bring peace to the region. It is interesting to recall a

---

1. Ibid.
2. Sir Knox Helm, Tel-Aviv to FO, 27 March 1951, FO 371/91368, document no. uncertain.
3. See, e.g., an interview given by the ex-Israeli president Ben-Zvi to *The Washington Post*, 4 December 1961.

point raised by one of the British officials during the debate about the transfer project: 'The scheme will accentuate the tendency of exaggerated nationalism, which is one of the main curses of the Middle East.'[1]

From the Israeli point of view, there was a clear connection between immigration and the need for expansion. Back in 1937 Golda Meir, the late Israeli prime minister, pointed out to her colleagues the connection between their demands for more immigrants and the need to expand: 'More population means more resources and more territories. Only wars change borders.'[2]

---

1. Cairo to FO, 22 September 1949, FO 371/75152, E 11995.
2. 'On the Ways of Our Policy', Report of the Congress of the World Council of Poale Zion held in Zurich from 29 July to 7 August 1937 (quoted by Woolfson, 1980, pp. 122–3).

FIVE

Exodus

The main concern of this chapter is to monitor and analyse the rapid and dramatic developments between March 1950, when the denaturalization law was passed, and July 1951, when nearly all the Jewish community left Iraq. What were the attitudes of different classes in the Jewish community towards emigration? Did the insecurity felt by the community after the establishment of Israel and the subsequent war itself account for the mass exodus? If not, what additional factors during the delicate period following the promulgation of Law 1/1950 might have triggered emigration on such a sweeping scale?

These questions have been examined by a number of authors, to whose work I shall refer briefly. But various British documents recently made available shed fresh light on the previously published material and clarify the circumstances of the exodus.

Latent Push Factors

Cases of mass emigration are often examined in the framework of 'push and pull' factors. Economic disadvantages and other negative features of life in the country of origin count as 'push' factors, which may be complemented by 'pull' factors like economic advantages and other opportunities in the host country. Political and religious pressures can also be accommodated. In his analysis of emigration to Israel by Arab Jews, 'Abd al-Majid (1978) extended this framework to include 'latent' push factors he saw as arising from the dependence of some minorities in the Arab world on colonial connections near the end of the nineteenth century. In the case of the Jews, any differences between their interests and those of other sections of Arab societies played no significant role until the outbreak of hostilities in Palestine. Indeed, according to 'Abd al-Majid, these latent push factors came forcefully to the surface only with the Zionist call, the Arab-Israeli conflict, and its aftermath. 'Abd al-Majid stresses two push factors: the misguided positions taken by some Arab governments and political groups holding religious or extreme nationalist views, and Jewish anxiety and insecurity largely fuelled by Zionist organizations. Pull factors, which he considers less important, were Israel's exploitation of the Jewish religion, the promises (prompted by the need for cheap labour) of a better economic life in Israel, and the influence of two major pieces of Israeli legislation: the Law of Return of 1950, which gave any Jew the right to emigrate to Israel and acquire immediate citizenship, and the Nationality Law of 1952.

Latent push factors may to some extent be traced to the general position of minorities in any society. 'Abd al-Majid argues that the insular tendency of Jewish communities was the main reason for their incomplete integration into the countries in which they lived. But this tendency, if it existed elsewhere, was less evident in the case of Arab Jews.

The latent push factors in Islamic societies can be traced to the beginning of the nineteenth century when these societies, to varying degrees, came under the influence of European colonial powers. Minorities in Islamic countries, Jews among them, tended to associate themselves with the expanding foreign interests. This trend was encouraged by the imposition of the Capitulation system. Minorities thus benefited from colonial domination, and bad feeling towards these minorities may be seen in part as one expression of widespread opposition to such domination. 'Landshut may well be right in arguing that the Capitulation system was the most important reason for the severance of ties between Jews and their social surroundings' ('Abd al-Majid, 1978, p. 42).

The fact that the interests of some Arab Jews were tied to the Capitulation system and later to Western imperialism as the guarantor of some of these privileges led, according to 'Abd al-Majid, to a conflict between sections of the Arab Jewish communities and the national independence movements – even though these movements often sought the support of minorities in creating national unity.

This conflict was clearest in Arab North Africa, where a large section of the Jewish community preferred the continuation of French rule. About a third of Tunisian Jews, for example, had French nationality, and many supported French rule (see Taymuni, 1982). Jewish support for the French was even stronger in Algeria, where many Jews had taken advantage of a French law of 1865 allowing any Jew in French territories to apply for French nationality. 'Abd al-Majid refers to a December 1958 report in the *Jewish Chronicle* (quoted by Schechtman, 1960) which estimated that 80 per cent of Algerian Jews wanted a French Algeria.[1] 'Abd al-Majid concludes that an analysis of waves of Jewish emigration from North Africa gives some credibility to this assessment of the Jews' attitude to France: Jewish emigration rose substantially as independence grew nearer.

The cautious or antagonistic attitude of Jews whose interests were tied to foreign privileges has, according to 'Abd al-Majid, deeper economic significance. The independence movements were led by sections of national capital, which represented a threat to the interests of the Jews. This can be seen in Egypt and Syria. Nationalist feelings ran high in the struggle for Egyptian independence, and these feelings were also directed against foreigners who were considered allies of the British and agents for the exploiting class that dominated economic life. Most Jews in Egypt were of foreign nationality. The 1947 census revealed that of

---

1. A later report in the *Jewish Chronicle* (12 February 1960) raised the estimate to 90 per cent.

65,639 Jews living in Egypt, only 5,000 were of Egyptian nationality (see Nassar, 1980, p. 13).

After the treaty of 1936 and the cancellation of foreign privileges under the Montreux treaty of 1937, a number of laws were passed giving the government some degree of control over foreign companies and interests and stipulating an increase in the number of their Egyptian employees. 'Some researchers have pointed out that Egyptian regulations designed to curtail foreign influence threatened the economic position of Jews and other foreign minorities. This was particularly the case with the Companies Act of July 1947, which required that 70 per cent of administrative and clerical staff, and 90 per cent of manual workers in all Egyptian establishments be of Egyptian nationality' ('Abd al-Majid, 1978, p. 44).

Unlike 'Abd al-Majid, I would argue that the case of Syrian Jews was different from that of Egypt. Syrian Jews were mostly indigenous, and their economic position did not worsen as a result of legislation. Competition from other sectors of national capital seems to have been a strong factor in the emigration of Jewish traders and merchants. According to Landshut (1950), the 1943 census put the number of Jews in Syria at 29,770. He estimates that 22,000 of them emigrated to the United States and Brazil, mainly in the mid-1940s.

Latent push factors, then, played a significant role in some Arab countries, and at least in Syria ceased to be latent before 1948. Thus, although they later interacted with the Palestinian conflict, they were initially independent of it. These latent factors led to some Jewish emigration, mainly to Europe and the Americas. There was also some internal migration within the Arab countries,[1] but migration to Palestine by Arab Jews was quite limited before 1948. But the latent

---

1. There was a small-scale Jewish migration, mainly from Syria, Palestine, and Iraq to Egypt, between the two world wars, mostly for economic reasons. The healthy economic position the Jews were able to maintain in Lebanon attracted others from Syria, Iraq, and Iran during the 1940s and 1950s. Between 1944 and 1958, the number of Jews living in Lebanon almost doubled. In 1958 there were 11,000 Jews, including 3,000 who had emigrated from Syria. (See Abdo and Kasmieh, 1971, pp. 41–9.)

push factors had far less impact in Iraq than in the Arab countries examined by 'Abd al-Majid. Iraqi Jews were well-integrated with other parts of society. They were mainly Iraqi nationals (very few foreign Jews had settled in Iraq), and although they benefited from commercial ties with foreign interests, they had enjoyed wealth and economic prominence well before European interests became significant.

Moreover, Iraqi Jews were able to maintain their economic prominence in independent Iraq right up to the time of their exodus. The expanding role of the (mainly Shi'i) Muslim merchants during the late thirties and forties was not accompanied by a deterioration of the economic conditions of Jewish traders (as had happened in Syria, for instance). Nor were any government restrictions affecting Jewish businesses imposed before 1948 (as had happened in Egypt). The economic prominence of Iraqi Jews might also be attributed to additional factors: British influence, which remained strong after independence; the monarchy's economic liberalism; and the close ties Jewish traders continued to maintain with people in power.

The upper strata of Jewish traders were subject to widespread criticism and resentment during the economic crisis of the second world war, but no government restrictions were imposed that might have seriously damaged Jewish businesses. Indeed, it is generally agreed that Jewish businesses experienced a boom for most of the 1940s. It was only after the Arab-Israeli war in 1948 that measures limiting Jewish prominence in trade were introduced, in particular after members of the Istiqlal Party joined the government of Nuri al-Said in 1949.

Competition from other sectors of national capital does not seem to have led to any significant Jewish emigration. Jewish traders displayed a remarkable ability to adapt and work in changing conditions. Many were partners with Muslims. The flourishing Baghdadi Jewish community in India had settled there before Iraq became independent, and many of these families not only established firms in Britain but also retained strong interests in Iraq.

The relative weakness of latent push factors is reflected in the fact that there were no large communities of Iraqi Jewish origin in

Europe or the Americas. Throughout the 1940s, while Syrian Jews were emigrating in their thousands, Iraqi Jews were buying land, building schools, and establishing new enterprises.

'Push and Pull' and the Arab-Israeli Conflict

The establishment of the state of Israel and the hostilities that followed had dramatic effects on the Arab Jews. Latent push factors were severely aggravated in most Arab societies. Paradoxically, it was in Iraq, where latent factors had been far less powerful than in other Arab countries, that the effects of the establishment of Israel were the most serious.

The repercussions of the war in Palestine and the activities of the Zionists definitely created insecurity and anxiety among the Jewish community in Iraq. This insecurity and anxiety was sometimes reinforced and sometimes countered by fleeting prospects for peace.

I have already alluded to the main factors contributing to the fluctuating feeling of insecurity in the Iraqi Jewish community. These factors, which all had to do with the aftermath of the Palestine war, included the attitudes of the Iraqi authorities, the restrictions and arrests of 1948–49, the skilful use of these events by Zionist activists, and the consequent weakening of the position of the Jewish community's leadership figures. Feelings of insecurity ebbed and flowed as the prospects for peace appeared better or worse. But the majority view probably persisted in regarding the difficulties as temporary. It was expected that when the restrictions were relaxed, the worst was over. Most Jews saw their future in Iraq and sought to accommodate to the new situation created by the establishment of the state of Israel.

This was also the view taken by prominent Jews and the leaders of the community. It was expressed by Senator Ezra Menahem Daniel in two speeches during the debate on the denaturalization bill. He devoted much time to defending the right of Iraqi Jews to stay and live as full Iraqi citizens. 'The bill', Daniel said, 'deals with only one aspect of the Jewish question in Iraq. What can be done to reassure the Jews who do not wish to leave their homeland for good and who are loyal and law-abiding citizens?'

Daniel questioned the wisdom of some of the administrative measures placing exceptional restrictions on Iraqi Jews after the war in Palestine. He argued:

> Does not the government consider it to be its duty to reassure this large section of loyal citizens by removing those extraordinary restrictions in order to restore to Iraqi Jews their sense of security, confidence, and stability? The Jews have lived in Iraq for 3,500 years; that is why they are reluctant to emigrate unless they are really obliged to do so.[1]

That reluctance to leave to which Daniel referred was understandable in a climate of optimism that some kind of peaceful settlement in Palestine was still possible. There is considerable evidence that the Iraqi government was in favour of such an early settlement, and the fate of the Iraqi Jews was never raised in any proposal put forward by Iraqi officials.[2]

Many sources indicate that Nuri al-Said (then Iraqi prime minister), perhaps more than any other Arab leader, was actively seeking accommodation with Israel, though he insisted on the repatriation of the Palestinian refugees. At one stage, he offered to place the areas of Palestine controlled by the Iraqi Army under UN supervision, even though these areas were supposed to be Arab according to UN partition resolutions.[3]

---

1. Baghdad to FO, 21 March 1950, FO 37a/82478, EQ 1571/17/50.
2. In the autumn of 1951, months after Law 5/1951 was passed, Nuri al-Said was approached with the idea of setting up a regional security pact under which Israel and Arab states would work together. It was reported that he was not opposed to making peace with Israel. Indeed he was prepared to allow Iraqi Jews to come back if a satisfactory peace was signed. (Baghdad to FO, 10 October 1951, FO 371/91368, EE 1072/29.)
3. Baghdad to FO, 29 March 1949, FO 371/75383.

According to Waldmar J. Gallman (1964), the American ambassador to Iraq between 1954 and 1958:

> The UN resolution of 1947 on partition was the starting point of Nuri's hopes for building a working relationship with Israel … He offered that there should be two states in Palestine, with Jerusalem as an open city (pp. 167, 225).

The connection between peace prospects in Palestine and Jewish emigration from Iraq was clearly strong. The American and British governments both regarded it as the major factor in their assessments of Jewish attitudes to emigration. Perhaps more important, these assessments were made only months after the war in Palestine, at a time when the Jewish community still faced the full effects of the restrictions the Iraqi government had imposed.

The American report of March 1949[1] was based on the assumption that active warfare in Palestine would soon cease and that some sort of settlement would be effected along the lines of the UN General Assembly resolution of 11 December 1948 (which called, among other things, for the right of return or compensation for the Palestinian refugees). The report dismissed the possibility of the large-scale emigration of Iraqi Jews. It characterized the Iraqi government's attitude to the Jews under the Pachachi and al-Said cabinets as 'reasonable and moderate' on the whole and noted that much of the anti-Jewish feeling of summer 1948 had receded.[2]

More significantly, the American report saw the prospect of the Jewish emigration as closely tied to the kind of policy Israel might pursue in the future. The report concluded:

> The desire of the Jewish community to emigrate will in great part be induced or limited by the amount of aggressiveness and recalcitrance which Israel may display in future. To the degree that stability in Palestine and the Middle East is

---

1. See Appendix 2.
2. Ibid.

disturbed by Israel's pursuance of a policy of expansionism, the Iraqi Jews will suffer more disabilities; the community as a whole might eventually come to welcome the possibility of emigration. If Israel, however, pursued a policy of moderation, and agreed to a peace settlement considered not too unreasonable by the Arabs, not more than a small proportion of Iraq's Jewish community would want to emigrate to Palestine.[1]

This assessment was shared by British officials a few months later, in the autumn of 1949, when the debate about the transfer scheme took place. The British ambassador in Tel-Aviv believed that 'unless persecution develops, the Iraqi Jews are probably better off in Iraq than they would be in Israel'.[2] Other British officials dismissed the possibility of any voluntary emigration under the proposed scheme. Some argued that the Iraqi Jews would suffer from the transfer, though they agreed that 'Israel would care little for the Iraqi Jews' hardships'.[3]

Following the establishment of Israel, Zionist activists began to operate among Jewish youth in Iraq, exploiting the general unease and claiming, according to Berger (1955), that 'American Jews were putting up large sums of money to take them to Israel where everything would be in apple-pie order' (p. 163).

The state of uncertainty that enveloped the business life of the Jewish community after 1948 was largely responsible for the stagnation of Iraq's economy. Less privileged families among the Jews were particularly affected. It was on this section of the community, especially the young, that the Zionists concentrated their efforts before the mass exodus. One of the Zionist emissaries involved in organizing the illegal emigration later explained:

---

1. Ibid.
2. FO to Baghdad, 11 November 1949, FO 371/76152, E 13371.
3. Ibid.

Our chief concern was to persuade the youth to settle in Palestine. For the most part, the middle-aged and older Jews had become reconciled to their lot, and it was next to impossible to wean them from the attitudes and habits of generations and to fire them with zest for a new life in the land of their fathers. The idea of beginning life afresh was a little too much for them. We usually had to accept that attitude, but not the assumption that the young people were satisfied with their lot and with the prospect of going on in their parents' immutable ways. We were determined to get them to Palestine and to a life of freedom and of work in the service of their natural homeland (Mardor, 1964, pp. 89–90).

The emigration of the young split the loyalties of their families and, given the strong family ties among Iraqi Jews, proved effective in attracting older people to follow at a later stage. Concern about family ties led some Iraqi senators to urge a cautious study of the denaturalization bill. One even argued that Iraqi nationality should be relinquished on a family rather than an individual basis.[1]

The number of those involved in illegal immigration before the denaturalization law was passed can only be guessed at. In March 1950 the Iraqi authorities estimated that about three thousand had left the country illegally. Hillel (1977, p. 102), however, claims that the Zionist movement succeeded in getting more than five thousand illegal emigrants to Israel. It is not clear if Hillel's figures also cover the period after Law 1/1950 was issued, for even after the law some of those who wanted to leave the country preferred to do so illegally. Usually these were people who wanted to evade the currency restrictions imposed a few weeks later, which allowed each emigrant to take only 50 dinars. Groups of Communist activists also preferred to leave the country illegally, to keep out of sight.

---

1. See, for instance, the comments made by Senator Mustafa al-Umari during the discussion of Bill 1/1950 (Baghdad to FO, 21 March 1950, FO 371/82478, EQ 1571/17/50).

Although Israeli official statistics report the number of Jews who arrived from Iraq each year, they do not distinguish between legal and illegal immigrants from the standpoint of Iraqi law (see Table 13).

Table 13: Immigrants from Iraq to Israel, 1948–53

Year	Number
1948	15
1949	1708
1950	32453
1951	89088
1952	961
1953	413
Total	124638

Source: Sicron (1957, p. 22).

Reliable sources among the community, however, estimated that by the end of 1950 some ten thousand Iraqi Jews had left the country illegally.[1]

It is hard to believe that Israel was a major pull factor to the Iraqi Jews, whether on ideological or economic grounds. Those who left illegally were mainly young people looking for fresh opportunities when prospects around them seemed bleak. Even then, many would have been unable to emigrate without active encouragement and support from Zionist activists and thus had no choice in determining their destination. Syrian Jews, who were less wealthy, did not find Israel a great attraction at the time. And of 27,000 Egyptian Jews who left the country between August and November 1949, only 7,268 settled in Israel (Schechtman, 1960, p. 192).

It is difficult to see the illegal emigration as the prelude to large-scale migration, let alone to a mass exodus. Emigration was a tough

---

1. See report written by Shaul Sasson, the son of the chief rabbi, presented to the British Embassy in Baghdad, dated 14 December 1950 (FO 371/82481, EQ 1571/58).

decision which the majority of Jews were reluctant to make. Their roots, culture, and livelihood lay in the country in which they had lived for centuries, while their future in Israel seemed no less uncertain than their conditions in Iraq.

Some of those who had already migrated wrote back to their relatives that they often found life in Israel disturbing and discouraging. Their letters referred to mounting difficulties in adapting to the new society and to acts of discrimination against them. It is hard to assess the effect of this factor, but Zionist and non-Zionist sources alike recognize that it did seriously influence the level of emigration from Iraq (see Cohen, 1969, pp. 138–41, and Darwish, 1981, p. 81).

For many individual Jews the decision to emigrate was largely determined by their social position. In general, in the case of the Iraqi as well as other Jewish communities, the wealthier and more established families were the last to leave, and when they did, Israel was not their first choice of destination. About 99 per cent of the nearly 150,000 Jews of Algeria and about 60 per cent of Tunisia's 100,000 Jews settled in Europe (see Chouraqui, 1968, and Schechtman, 1960).

Less privileged families generally found it easier to take the decision to emigrate, and many of these settled in Israel. Most of the Syrian, Egyptian, Moroccan, and Tunisian Jews of this social category did so. The early Zionist success in attracting members of the less privileged and more backward communities among the Kurds, Yemenis, and Moroccans can be understood in the light of the limited choices these communities had.

The emigration of upper- and middle-class Iraqi Jews to Israel therefore represents an unusual case which invites careful examination. It is true that people of this social category were also to be found among the Libyan Jews, who, like the Iraqis, emigrated *en masse* to Israel (reportedly 35,142 in all). But this took place much later, between 1956 and 1958, after a new round of Arab-Israeli hostilities, and can probably be explained by the fact that few Libyan

Jews were of foreign nationality, unlike other Jews of North Africa. The more wealthy and those with Italian passports stayed behind.[1]

Only a year before Law 1/1950 was passed, the American report of March 1949[2] offered a rare assessment of the attitude of Iraqi Jews to emigration. It pointed to clear variances depending on social category.

Older religious leaders, rabbis, and their followers, the report suggested, would not want to give up their established positions in Iraq in exchange for an unpredictable future in Palestine. Leaders of the Jewish financial and business community, who were Europeanized to a large extent, would probably be divided: those who had identified emotionally with the Zionist state or who had exaggerated fears of possible Iraqi action against them would want to go to Palestine, even if considerable sacrifice was involved; those who had not identified with the Zionist state and who regarded themselves as Iraqis (perhaps the majority of this category) would prefer to maintain their comparatively comfortable and economically privileged positions in Iraq.

The American report predicted that many younger men of the 'white collar' class, those under thirty who were not yet firmly established in their economic activities, would be interested in emigrating to Israel in the belief that they would have better opportunities there than in Iraq. Many of the several hundred officials discharged from government employment in Iraq or from such institutions as Basra Port Authority and the Iraq Petroleum Company as a result of Iraq's involvement in the Palestine war would wish to emigrate to Israel. Finally, small tradesmen, artisans, and so on were unlikely to be interested in moving to Israel unless the community's religious and economic leaders made active efforts to persuade them.

The report's assessment of the attitude of Iraqi Jews to emigration was largely realistic for its time. Very little would have changed when the denaturalization law was passed the following

---

1. For details see 'Institute of Jewish Affairs', June and August 1967.
2. See Appendix 2.

year. Iraqi and British official sources all dismissed the possibility of a large-scale emigration. In fact, not more than ten to fifteen thousand Jews were expected to leave, no more than 10 per cent of the community.

In its report on the passing of Law 1/1950, *The Times* (4 March 1950) wrote that it was unlikely that the established Jews of Iraq would wish to leave, but: 'It is possible that there may be an exodus of the poorer Jews.' This view was shared by British officials in Baghdad. When a British airline offered to evacuate up to 40,000 Jews, the high commissioner wrote to London (on 13 April 1950, five weeks after the passing of Law 1/1950 and a few days after the first bomb attack against the Jews, which we will discuss later): 'We don't believe that as many as 40,000 will wish to go.'[1]

The denaturalization law was a unique piece of legislation in the Arab world. No other Arab country had given its Jewish citizens such an irrevocable choice about their nationality and destination (Yemeni Jews had no choice in the latter). All contemporary assessments indicate that the numbers expected to emigrate fell far short of those who actually did so.

It might therefore be concluded that neither the immediate repercussions in Iraq of the proclamation of Israel nor the passing of Law 1/1950 fully accounts for large-scale emigration of the Jewish community, let alone the mass exodus that in fact occurred. The time limit within which the decision to leave had to be made, however, did present opportunities to exploit events.

An examination of Jewish emigration from Egypt, another independent Arab country which, like Iraq, went to war with Israel, supports this view. About fifty thousand Egyptian Jews, or two-thirds of the community there, stayed in Egypt until the 1956 war. The comparison seems more significant in the light of several other factors as well: Zionist influence among the Egyptian Jewish community was traditionally far stronger than in Iraq; most Egyptian Jews were of foreign nationalities and were subjected to acts of violence on at least two occasions, in 1945 and 1948; the emergence

---

1. Baghdad to FO, 13 April 1950, FO 371/82480, EQ 1571/17.

of Arab nationalism under Nasser after 1952 would not have been welcomed by most Egyptian Jews; religious groups like the Muslim Brotherhood were active in Egypt but not in Iraq.

To understand the circumstances that made the mass exodus of Iraqi Jews possible, one must examine carefully the events that followed the passing of Law 1/1950. These events, combined with the factors discussed earlier, finally led to something approaching mass hysteria. Two developments were of particular importance, and seem to have seriously stimulated Jewish emigration. First, on 7 May 1950 an agreement on transport arrangements between al-Suwaidi, the Iraqi prime minister, and Shlomo Hillel, a Zionist delegate, virtually placed the evacuation in the hands of the Israeli authorities. Second, about the time Hillel was in Baghdad negotiating the evacuation deal a series of bomb attacks on Jewish targets began. These attacks worsened during the first half of 1951.

The Hillel-Suwaidi Evacuation Deal

Shlomo Hillel was an Iraqi Jew who settled in Palestine and became active with Mossad, the secret service. He made more than one trip to Iraq to organize illegal emigration before he was sent to Baghdad at the end of March 1950 to make arrangements to transport to Israel those who decided to leave in accordance with Law 1/1950. Hillel was officially acting as a representative of an American registered company called Near East Air Transport, Inc. (NEATI), which was in fact owned by the Jewish Agency and had been set up by the Zionist movement to fly Jewish immigrants to Israel. A few months earlier the company had been involved in the evacuation of the Yemeni Jews.

Hillel's version (1977) of his visit to Baghdad reads like a spy story that strains credulity. It is unlikely that the Iraqi authorities failed, as he claimed, to recognize him or his company even after he had spent nearly five weeks in Baghdad and had met with al-Suwaidi in two private sessions. Hillel was from Baghdad and his family still lived there; neither his looks nor his accent could have supported his claim to be an American. Moreover, he had previously been arrested by the Iraqi authorities for his Zionist activities.

In fact, Hillel's visit and his later deal with al-Suwaidi is the main evidence marshalled by supporters of the theory that the entire affair, including Law 1/1950, was the result of a conspiracy between Iraqi and Israeli officials. But there is no evidence to suggest that there was any Israeli-Iraqi communication, direct or indirect, before Hillel's visit to Baghdad. Moreover, it is important to remember that it took Hillel nearly a month in Baghdad to conclude the transport arrangements with al-Suwaidi. Indeed, it is more likely that the Iraqi authorities and Jewish community leaders were discussing various transport arrangements for those who wanted to leave well before Hillel's visit.[1]

It is also dubious whether al-Suwaidi's government could have reached an understanding with the Zionists on the evacuation arrangements at an earlier stage without the consent, or at least the knowledge, of the British. It is significant that news of Hillel's deal with al-Suwaidi was first received by the Foreign Office from the British legation in Tel-Aviv and not from Baghdad. A copy of the agreement was given to Sir Knox Helm in Tel-Aviv, a few days after it was concluded by the Israeli Foreign Office.[2] The agreement was signed on 7 May 1950. The Foreign Office was told:

> The Near East Air Transport, Inc. United States air company is making an agreement with the Iraqi government for the evacuation by air of Jews from Iraq provided that they be landed in the first instance in the territory of a state with which Iraq has normal diplomatic relations.
>
> It is understood that this provision will be met by technical landing at Nicosia in Cyprus and that the authorities will immediately be approached about this through American channels.

---

1. FO 371/8249, EQ 1571/16.
2. Tel-Aviv to FO, 12 May 1950, FO 371/82480, EQ 1571/20.

The Israeli government will grant entry permits to all Jewish passengers flown by the above-named company from Baghdad to Lydda via Nicosia.[1]

The question to be answered is this: what influenced the al-Suwaidi government to make such an arrangement with Hillel? All the indications are that the Israelis relied on two factors: American help and bribery of senior Iraqi officials, including al-Suwaidi himself.

Recently available evidence shows that the Zionists were increasingly relying on rising American influence in the region to achieve their ends. It now seems certain that the Americans, and not (as is widely believed) the British, played the major role in this last episode of the Jewish exodus from Iraq. Americans, for instance, acted as the sponsors for Hillel's mission, and they seem to have used their influence on all parties involved, including the British, to facilitate it.

In a telegram dated 29 March 1950, the day Hillel arrived in Baghdad, the British ambassador to Washington told London:

> The American Joint Distribution Committee has suggested to the State Department that they be permitted to send a discreet (unofficial) representative to Iraq with a view to organizing the emigration of Iraqi Jews to Israel in conjunction with competent Iraqi officials. The State Department is sympathetic to this proposal, and has asked the United States Embassy in Baghdad to approach it informally in their discussion with the Iraqis … The State Department expressed the hope that His Majesty's ambassador in Baghdad might support this suggestion if his views are sought by the Iraqis.[2]

The dilemma of the British is illustrated by frequent statements in FO correspondence with the legation in Baghdad. For example: 'We

---

1. Ibid.
2. Washington to FO, 29 March 1950, FO 371/82479, EQ 1571/1.

don't want to get ourselves in the position of representing Israeli interests in Iraq.' This is a clear reference to the position taken by the Americans. The FO kept advising its legation to undertake 'close consultation' with the Americans. The British subsequently expressed no objection to the American request to facilitate Hillel's mission.[1]

When asked later what advice it could offer concerning the Iraqi decision to freeze Jewish property, the FO wrote back to Baghdad

> I think that we should instruct H. M. Chargé d'Affaires in Baghdad to extend the evacuation period ... This approach should be made in close consultation with his American colleague, and I think it is very important that we should keep closely in step with the Americans over this matter.[2]

Evidence also shows that the American legations in Baghdad, Tehran, and Cyprus were in constant contact with the State Department to help in finalizing arrangements for the departure of the Iraqi Jews. The legations in both Tehran and Cyprus were instructed to secure visas for immigrants, while the legation in Baghdad reported the increasing rate of registration to Washington on a day-to-day basis.[3]

Foreign Office documents show that the British, who were already losing influence, made no secret of their displeasure that NEATI had obtained a monopoly of transporting the Jewish emigrants. British companies complained that the Iraqi authorities were discriminating against them. Efforts by the British government to support British companies in their attempt to secure a share in the operation failed. What might be seen as commercial competition soon blossomed into a political row with the Israelis, backed by the Americans on

1. FO to Baghdad, telegram no. 74, 6 April 1950, FO 371/82479. Also: Baghdad to FO, 13 April 1950, FO 371/82480, EQ 1571/7.
2. FO to Baghdad, 22 March 1951, FO 371/91690.
3. Baghdad to FO, date unclear, April 1950, FO 371/8248, EQ 1571/19.

one side and the British on the other.[1] Iraqi officials seemed most interested in their own personal stake in matters, with al-Suwaidi, the prime minister, and Saleh Jabr, the interior minister, supporting the deal concluded with NEATI.

There were many rumours that financial arrangements had been made to persuade al-Suwaidi and Jabr to agree to the deal, rumours that were never confirmed by Iraqi or Israeli officials. Nevertheless, there are strong hints in Hillel's account (1977, pp. 94, 104–05) that both al-Suwaidi and Jabr benefited personally from the decision to grant the evacuation contract to NEATI. Hillel recalled that during his meeting with al-Suwaidi he promised the prime minister a 'big share in profits' and that they agreed to pay the Iraqi government £14 sterling per ticket. 'We parted', Hillel wrote, 'on the most cordial terms.'

Meanwhile, in a lengthy confidential letter summing up developments in the transportation row, the British high commissioner in Baghdad wrote to London:

> As a result of enquiries which were made of the Iraqi authorities, the difficulties of the British operators appeared to derive from the fact that the American firm (NEATI) had ignored the usual procedures of submitting an application through the Civil Aviation Committee and had gone 'right to the top'.[2]

Later in the letter, Sir Henry Mack revealed that NEATI was operating through a local travel agency, Iraq Tour, in which al-Suwaidi owned an interest.

---

1. The British tried to exert pressure by denying NEATI permission to land in Cyprus. The Israelis, in return, made it clear that they would not allow any other company to land in Israel. The Americans supported the Israelis, and pressed the British to allow NEATI to land in Cyprus. But the issue soon became irrelevant as the flights started to leave Baghdad directly for Israel (FO 371/82482, EQ 1571/28. Also: FO 371/82486, EQ 1371/59.)
2. Baghdad to FO, 5 June 1950, FO 371/82482, EQ 1571/28.

The possibility of personal benefit might also explain, at least partially, Nuri al-Said's determination to expedite the evacuation. He was out of the cabinet when al-Suwaidi concluded the evacuation deal with Hillel, but when al-Said took over the premiership in September 1950, he tried unsuccessfully to give the British companies a share in the evacuation operation. Among these companies was BOAC, for which al-Said's son was acting as agent.[1]

It is not clear whether al-Said derived any personal benefit. Israel, for its part, moved to meet his demand to expedite the evacuation by deciding, on 15 October 1950, to increase the number of NEATI flights to two a day. No British company was allowed to share the traffic. The following year allegations of corruption were made in the Iraqi Senate against four ministers, among them al-Suwaidi, al-Said, and Jabr. Some Iraqi newspapers, as well as British officials, pointed out that 'there is no doubt that the charges had some substance'.[2] Furthermore, during the trials held after the revolution of 14 July 1958, which brought down the monarchy, allegations of personal benefit from the evacuation deal with Hillel were made against al-Suwaidi (see accounts of al-Suwaidi's trial, Mahkamat al-Sha'b, 1959).

'Cruel Zionism'

Another series of events that had far-reaching consequences in the Jewish emigration were the bomb attacks in Baghdad. A few weeks after the denaturalization law was passed, and around the time Hillel was discussing the evacuation arrangements with al-Suwaidi, the first of a series of bombs against Jewish targets was detonated.

On 8 April 1950 a hand grenade exploded in Abu Nuwas Street near a coffee house frequented by Jews. A number of people were

---

1. It was reported that in his attempts to win a share in the operation al-Said's son promised that BOAC could transfer 50,000 Jews directly to Israel within a month in order to expedite the evacuation. See H. Beely, letter to FO, 20 December 1950, FO 371/82486, EQ 1371/50.
2. Baghdad to FO, 6 June 1951, FO 371/91633.

injured but no one was killed. On 14 January 1951 a second hand grenade exploded near Mas'uda Shemtob Synagogue, killing two passing Muslims and injuring a number of Jews who had gathered near the synagogue. On 14 March 1951 a third bomb exploded, this time at the US Information Centre building opposite Suq al-Saffarin in Rashid Street, a centre frequented by large numbers of Jews. A few visitors to the centre were injured but no one was killed. On the night of 10 May, there was an explosion in the Lawy building, owned by a Jewish car dealer. No one was hurt, but there was some damage to the building itself. On 5 June 1951, at night, there was an explosion near the building of the Jewish firm of Stanly Sha'ashoua, causing no damage. (For more details see: al-Hasani, 1955b, p. 193, and Haim, 1978, pp. 199–200).

No one was identified as responsible for these attacks, and a state of anxiety persisted for nearly a year after the first bomb, until 26 June 1951, when the Iraqi government issued a communiqué stating that it had uncovered 'a spy ring in Baghdad run by two foreigners who had been arrested' (the reference is to Yehuda Tajjar, an Israeli officer, and a British subject called Rodney, who was actually a Mossad agent), together with most of their associates, including those responsible for the series of explosions.

The authorities also discovered explosives, files, typewriters, presses, and membership lists hidden in synagogues or buried in private houses. These were seized in the presence of the judge in charge of the investigation, the Baghdad chief of police, and a group of Jewish notables. The purpose of the terrorist acts, according to the authorities, was three-fold:

(a) To terrorize the Jews and force them to emigrate to Israel, which they did in fact achieve.
(b) To exploit these acts in order to spread adverse propaganda against Iraq.
(c) To arouse the interest of the British and the Americans in the relations between the Jews and the Arabs. (Quoted by al-Hasani, 1955b, pp. 192–5.)

During the trial, the English-language *Iraq Times* of 20 December 1951 reported that documents seized were read in court. Some of these shed light on the organizational side of the Zionist movement in Iraq. One revealed that about three hundred youths between the ages of 13 and 18 had received military training. According to the notebook of one of the accused,

> The circular, which has been published and distributed to TNUA members, had good effect too on the Jewish community. Some Jews were formerly making secret propaganda for remaining, and objected to emigration, but within a month, there has been no effect left of their propaganda. And I would thank from my heart all members of TNUA … etc. (*Iraq Times*, 20 December 1951.)

A copy of a leaflet, said to have been distributed by the Zionists after the bomb attacks, was read in court. The leaflet warned the Jewish community of the consequences if they stayed in Iraq, and advised the Jews to return to 'their natural homeland, Israel'. The leaflet concluded, 'O sons of Zion, inhabitants of Babylon, free yourselves … O brother Jews, Israel is calling you.'[1]

Zionist propaganda fed the confusion caused by the failure of the Iraqi authorities to find those responsible for the bombings. Rumours spread, first in Baghdad, that Communists might be behind them. After the arrests, the World Jewish Congress (WJC) wrote to the Foreign Office stating that 'Muslim brothers *must be* responsible'. British officials, however, felt that the seized documents and arms, with the confessions and trial, 'left no room for doubt who were behind the bombs'. On 31 December 1951 the Foreign Office wrote to Sir Anthony Nutting, then inquiring into the affair: 'The WJC allegations were without any supporting evidence,

---

1. A hand-written leaflet, original copies found in the files of the Criminal Investigation Department, Baghdad. (Quoted by Abdul-Jabbar, head of Baghdad police.)

and they have no indications that the trials have in any way been improperly conducted.'[1]

This opinion was later endorsed by Wilbur Grane Eveland, a former adviser to the US Central Intelligence Agency (CIA) who was in Baghdad at the time. In his account of the bomb attacks, Eveland gave an insight into the positions taken by the Iraqi Jewish community, the Zionists, and the State Department. He wrote in his book *Ropes of Sand* (1980):

> Just after I arrived in Baghdad, an Israeli citizen had been recognized … his interrogation led to the discovery of fifteen arms caches brought into Iraq by the underground Zionist movement.
>
> … In an attempt to portray the Iraqis as anti-American and to terrorize the Jews, the Zionists planted bombs in the US Information Service Library and synagogues, and soon leaflets began to appear urging Jews to flee to Israel. Embarrassed, the Iraqi government launched a full-scale investigation, and shared its findings with our Embassy.
>
> Iraqi Chief Rabbi Sassoon Khedouri frequently came to see us at the Embassy. He was urging his people to be calm and remain, remembering that they were native Iraqis first and that Judaism was only their religion, which they could practice freely as always. In spite of our constant reports that the situation in Iraq was exaggerated and artificially inflamed from without, the State Department urged us to intervene with the government to facilitate an air-lift that the Zionists were organizing to 'rescue' Iraqi Jews … Although the Iraqi police later provided our Embassy with evidence to show that the synagogue and the library bombing, as well as the anti-Jewish and anti-American leaflet campaign, had been the work of an underground Zionist organization, most of the world believed reports that Arab terrorism had motivated the

---

1. P. A. Rhodes for the FO to Sir Anthony Nutting, 31 December 1951, FO 371/48767, EQ 1571/2.

flight of Iraqi Jews, whom the Zionists had 'rescued' really just in order to increase the Israeli Jewish population ... (pp. 48–9).

Understandably, Israeli official sources never admitted responsibility for the bomb attacks, and Israeli writers who had access to Zionist archives and wrote the history of the Zionist movement in Iraq generally did so from an official point of view. They either claimed that the available evidence did not enable them to make any judgement on this matter (for instance, Cohen, 1969), or seemed unconcerned with the matter (Me'ir, 1973; Atlas, 1969; Hillel, 1977).[1]

Subsequently released information about the bombs in Baghdad confirms the responsibility of the Zionist movement. The Israeli weekly *Ha'olam Hazeh* (29 May 1966) published an account of the emigration of the Iraqi Jews based on Tajjar's testimony. *Black Panther* magazine, a militant journal of Israeli oriental Jews, published the full story of the bombs and the Zionist activists who were behind them in its 9 November 1972 issue. The magazine's account includes the testimony of eyewitnesses. Both accounts were quoted fully by Woolfson (1980, pp. 189–201) and Hirst (1977, pp. 155–63).

On 5 November 1951 an Iraqi court found fifteen of the twenty-one defendants guilty and acquitted the rest. Yehuda Tajjar was sentenced to hard labour for life.[2] Shlomo Salih Shalom and Yusif Basri, both Iraqis, were sentenced to death and later executed. The other convicted defendants got terms of imprisonment varying between five months and fifteen years.

Two final points about the bombings should be made. The first concerns the failure of the Iraqi authorities to arrest those responsible for the earlier attacks. The perpetrators were discovered

---

1. Cohen did mention that Zionist leaflets were distributed at the time to encourage Jews to leave.
2. Tajjar was released ten years later and made his way back to Israel, where he joined the Foreign Ministry. He served as a cultural attaché in the Israeli Embassy in London in the early 1980s.

by accident,[1] and only when the evacuation of the Jews was nearing its end. This could be attributed to the incompetence and general lack of efficiency of the security forces. But the possibility cannot be ruled out that senior Iraqi officials preferred to close their eyes to the Zionist activities while the evacuation was under way. The reports of personal benefits and the release soon after his arrest of a local Zionist commander, Mordechai Ben-Porat,[2] described by many Israeli sources as the ring-leader of the bombing campaign, lends some credibility to this view.

Second, recent Israeli archival material shows that at least as early as 1942, the Jewish leadership in Palestine formulated a plan for the massive immigration of Arab Jews to Palestine and the Iraqi Jews were their first target. Yehouda Shenhav, an Associate Professor at the Department of Sociology and Anthropology in Tel-Aviv University, published an interesting article in *Social Identities* (2002: 522–45) based on these archival documents in which he referred to a so-called 'plan of the million' that was presented by Ben-Gurion to experts at a meeting in Rehvot in 1942. The plan went into considerable detail about routes to be taken, absorption services, clothing, medical treatment, shipments, vocational training for the new immigrants, and the food the new immigrants would receive based on caloric needs. The plan further included the architectural design of the immigrant camps, specifying the optimal size and style

1. Yehuda Tajjar, who had been sent to Baghdad for this mission, was recognized by a Palestinian Arab refugee who used to serve coffee in the military police station in Acre, where Tajjar had been an officer.
2. More information about Porat's involvement was brought to light in a disturbing article by Baruch Nadil, an Israeli journalist. See Woolfson, 1980, pp. 196–200. Porat, whose Iraqi name was Murad Kazzaz, later served as a member of the Knesset before he lost his seat in the 1984 elections. He acted as a president of a group called World Organization for Jews from Arab Countries, set up in Israel in an attempt to counter-balance Palestinian claims. On the eve of the Islamic revolution in Iran, Porat was sent to Tehran to encourage the emigration of the Jewish community to Israel.

of the buildings, the type of lumber to be used for construction, and the provision of basic equipment and sanitation facilities.[1]

Information about the Iraqi and other Jewish communities in the region used in developing the plan was gathered through impressions gleaned by emissaries who were working for the Jewish construction company Solel Boneh in coordination with the British colonial administration – it has a large presence in Abadan and branches in the region included Bahrain, Beirut, Baghdad and Damascus at the time, as well as by the special Jewish military units who served in the region as part of the British army. Shenhav believes that although the plan was not implemented immediately and contained some unfeasible provisions, 'it marked the start of a discourse and the initial spotlighting of Arab-Jews as a potential candidates for immigration to Palestine '.[2]

Ben-Gurion was a committed advocate to the transfer 'solution' which is based on expelling the Palestinian Arabs and replacing them by Jewish immigrants. He actually endorsed 'forced transfer' as seen in his diary entry for 12 July 1937 and other numerous personal and official documents later on as quoted by Masalha (2003, p.17–32). Based on the released Zionist archive, Masalha analyses Israeli policies towards Palestinian refugees as they evolved since the Zionist scheme started in the 1920s. He has described these policies as classic cases of denial: the denial that Zionist 'transfer committees' were in operation between 1937 and 1948, aiming to forcibly expel Palestinians and prevent their return; denial of their right to restitution for their usurped properties and indeed denial of any responsibility for the refugee problem whatsoever.[3]

While acknowledging the early work of the modern Israeli historian Benny Morris (1987) in investigating the circumstances that

1. Shenhav, Yahouda (2002): The Phenomenology of Colonialism and the Politics of 'Difference': European Zionist Emissaries and Arab-Jews in Colonial Abadan, *Social Identities*, vol. 8, no. 4, 2002, pp. 522–45, Taylor & Francis, Carefax Publishing.
2. Ibid., p. 522.
3. Masalaha, Nur (2003): *The Politics of Denial: Israel and the Palestinian Problem*, Pluto Press, London.

led to the creation of the Palestinian refugee problem, Masalha makes a strong critique of Morris's works, which compile and document cases of expulsion of Palestinians at the hands of the Zionist militias, but stop short of acknowledging that these were not separated cases but part of master plan to force the Palestinians out. 'How can Morris be so categorical in stating that there was no Israeli expulsion policy when many relevant Israeli files and documents, both classified and publicly available, including some used by Morris himself, indicate otherwise?' Masalha asks.[1] He discusses various Israeli schemes to resettle Palestinian refugees permanently in neighbouring Arab states, including Iraq and other locations. 'If you can't solve it, dissolve it' is how a senior Israel official summarises Israeli attitudes in the 1950s following the exodus.[2] Masalha came to the conclusion that about 80 per cent of Palestinians were driven out of their land, that was occupied by the Israelis in 1948–49, mainly by psychological warfare and/or military pressure.[3]

There is reason to believe that the bombings could not have been carried out without a decision taken at a high level in Tel-Aviv. Three senior officers Yigal Allon, Yitzhak Rabin and Moshe Dayan, who were fostered by Ben-Gurion at the time, carried out the expulsion of large numbers of Palestinians from Lydda and Ramle at gunpoint in July 1948. At least two of these officers, Allon and Dayan, were also involved in recruiting and overseeing Zionist underground activities in Iraq and supervising recruits like Ben-Porat and Shlomo Hillel, both of whom are Iraqis. Allon was in charge of the external operations of Mossad and was in constant touch with Zionist activists in Baghdad, giving them instructions and supplying them with arms (Allon, 1970, pp. 233–4). Ben-Gurion, who fostered Ben-Porat's political career, showed personal interest in similar acts of violence. This was proved two years later, in July 1954, when Mossad agents launched a series of bomb attacks against American and British property in Egypt in what came to be known as the

---

1. Ibid., p. 54.
2. Ibid., p. 3.
3. Ibid., p. 29.

'Lavon Affair', which forced Ben-Gurion's resignation as prime minister.

The Israeli defence minister, commenting on the 'Lavon Affair', indirectly admitted the involvement of the Israeli government in the bombings in Iraq: 'This method of operation was not invented for Egypt. It was first tried in Iraq' (quoted by Woolfson, 1980, p. 199). Such anti-Jewish acts by Zionists in an attempt to force the emigration of Jewish communities to Israel has been termed 'cruel Zionism'. The term is attributed to Ben-Gurion himself.

It is obvious that the bombings came at a crucial time, when other factors seemed insufficient to ensure a mass exodus. The bombs brought all the various reasons for suspicion, fear, and anxiety into focus. It took the Iraqi authorities fourteen months to arrest those responsible, long enough to put tremendous pressure on the Jewish community and too long to be reassuring. Every time fears would abate, a new bomb shattered the feeling of security, and the prospect of staying on in Iraq seemed gloomier.

On the other hand, Law 1/1950 was supposed to expire a year after its passage. Given all the pressures and anxieties, the time limit of the new law acted as a catalyst for many Jews, precipitating their decision to leave. Most would have preferred to postpone any such decision, as other Arab Jewish communities generally did. It made very little difference that the denaturalization law was later extended, as most Iraqi Jews had by then already relinquished their nationality and had either left or were awaiting evacuation.

It also seems clear that the Zionists believed that the deadline for Law 1/1950 was final, and this conviction seems to have given them the sense that they were racing against time. According to Cohen (1969, pp. 192–3), the Zionists were eager to see the Iraqi Jews out of the country, or at least registered for leaving, before March 1951, the original expiry date for Law 1/1950.

The whole scene approached something like mass hysteria. With the bombings stirring ever greater fear and anxiety, the deadline of Law 1/1950 drew closer and closer, and evacuation looked like the only real possibility for those who felt the increasing pressure. Only the Yemeni Jews shared the fate of the Iraqis in having almost no element of choice in when and where to emigrate. Foreign Office documents, for instance, show that the British government advised its legation in Baghdad not to issue visas to Iraqi Jews. It took a few months of discussion before the Home Office agreed to allow eighty of them to continue to stay in Britain.[1]

With the imposition of the currency limit and the reluctance of other countries to receive them, all the Iraqi Jews who relinquished their nationality had no choice but to go to Israel. The al-Suwaidi government was well aware of the destination of the flights. The last provision of the evacuation deal was a formality to spare the Iraqi authorities any embarrassment. Later, in March 1951, the government stipulated its indifference to direct flights to Israel, 'so long as this was not admitted in writing'.[2]

Many Jews felt that the Iraqi authorities had not only failed to deal properly with the bombings or to give assurances to those Jews who wanted to stay, but also, by agreeing to the evacuation deal with NEATI, had showed for the first time that they were prepared to deal with Israel in matters concerning the community.

Zionist supporters, who previously had lacked influence in the community, suddenly became people to be feared, and consulted. While the future looked uncertain to many Jews, the Zionists seemed increasingly confident and well-informed about events. Some Iraqi Jews recall that colleagues of theirs who happened to have connections with the Zionist underground were able to forecast developments concerning the community (Bar-Moshe, 1975, pp. 538–9). Others pointed out that Zionist activists worked almost openly with Iraqi officials, while the community leadership was kept in the dark (Hillel, 1977, pp. 103–04).

The evidence shows that the Jewish community was the last to be consulted on the arrangements made for its departure. According to British sources, when the American Embassy sounded out Jewish opinion in Baghdad a few weeks before the Hillel-Suwaidi deal was

---

1. FO to Baghdad, 29 September 1952, FO 371/98767, EQ 1571/24.
2. Baghdad to FO, 6 June 1950, FO 371/82482, EQ 1571/28.

concluded, it found that the Jewish community would have preferred that 'no outside organization should come to Iraq to assist in the emigration'.[1] This was a coded reference to the Zionist organization. The community's view had special importance in this case, as it preceded Hillel's visit, or at least came while he was still in Baghdad negotiating with Iraqi officials. The Jews soon came to realize, however, that the Zionists actually had the upper hand in this last episode of their life in Iraq.

According to Foreign Office documents, when various means of transport were under discussion prior to Hillel's visit to Baghdad, Saleh Jabr, the interior minister, raised no objection to a proposal put forward by members of the Jewish community that they might charter a ship to transport Jews from the port of Basra.[2] Yet when community leaders approached the Iraqi government with a similar proposal in late May 1950, a few weeks after the Hillel-Suwaidi deal, the government refused to allow Jews 'to act as a community'.[3]

The effect of the bombings on Jewish emigration was unmistakable. Although official Iraqi sources give no day-to-day figures on the number who relinquished their nationality and left the country between 15 March 1950 (the first day for registration) and 5 July 1951 (by when all those who had registered had arrived in Israel), various other sources and cross-references allow us to draw the following conclusions.

Very few Jews registered during the first three weeks – that is, before the first terrorist bomb (at al-Bayda coffee house on 8 April 1950). Only three people turned up to register on the first day.[4] In all, 126 had registered before the attack (Sudani, 1980, p. 224, based on official Iraqi figures). Zionists have repeatedly claimed that Jews were reluctant to register at first because of their fear of the authorities (see, for example, Murad, 1977, p. 51). But since the Iraqi decision was long expected by the Zionists (see Bar-Moshe, 1975, pp. 538–9), this claim seems doubtful.

1. Baghdad to FO, 13 April 1950, FO 371/82480, EQ 1571/17.
2. Baghdad to FO, 1 April 1950, FO 371/8249, EQ 1571/16.
3. Baghdad to FO, 26 May 1950, FO 371/8248, EQ 1571/21.
4. FO 371/82482, EQ 1571/28

Almost immediately after the first bomb attack, thousands of Jews began to queue up in the registration offices, including 3,400 who registered on the day after the bombing (see Cohen, 1969, pp. 193–4, based on figures from the Jewish Agency). By 26 April 1950, about three weeks after the attack, 23,000 had completed the first stage of registration and 2,300 the second stage. By the end of 1950 it was reported that 31,500 of those who had registered had arrived in Israel.[1]

There is some evidence, however, that the rate of registration decelerated from the summer of 1950 to the end of the year. Nearly nine months passed before the second bombing, the one at Mas'uda Shemtob Synagogue on 14 January 1951. According to Foreign Office reports, at least 30,000 Jews had indicated their wish to stay in Iraq.[2] In its annual report for 1950, the Jewish Agency put the number of Iraqi Jews who were expected to come to Israel in 1951 at not more than 15,000.[3] Adding this to the number who had already left for Israel in 1950 (31,500), we find that 46,500 had already left or were ready to do so, of a community of about 130,000 in all.

The effect of the second terrorist attack was more serious. Here, unlike in the first case, a Jewish centre had clearly been targeted, and the first deaths occurred. During the six weeks prior to this attack, 2,300 had registered, as compared with 7,600 in the fortnight following the attack.[4]

By 8 March 1951, when the deadline for registration was supposed to expire, 105,000 Jews had registered and 40,000 had already left.[5] The deadline was later extended.

---

1. Report written by S. Sasson, 14 December 1950, FO 371/82481, EQ 1571/58. Also FO 371/91751, EQ 1571/2.
2. Ibid.
3. FO 371/91751, EQ 1571/2.
4. FO 371/91751, EQ 1571/2. Also FO 371/91691, EQ 1571/25.
5. Figures supplied to the British by the Iraqi Ministry of the Interior (FO 371/91690, EQ 1571/30).

The March 1951 attack on the US Information Centre was probably an attempt to portray the Iraqis as anti-American and to gain more support for the Zionist cause in the United States.

The last two attacks, in May and June 1951, were directed against Jewish firms. They were probably intended to put pressure on well-established members of the community, who were the last to emigrate.

By 5 July 1951 nearly all of those who had registered (105,000) had arrived in Israel. According to Israeli statistics, 124,646 Iraqi-born Jews arrived in Israel between the establishment of the state and the end of 1953. According to the 1957 Iraqi census, 4,906 Jews were still living in the country.

Those who stayed behind were among the best-established and most highly integrated members of the community. The majority of them left Iraq at a later stage, mainly for Europe and America.[1] All indications are that those who could afford to choose their destination preferred to settle in countries other than Israel. There are no precise figures of how many succeeded in doing so, but there is reason to believe that not less than 10,000 Iraqi Jews settled outside Israel in the early 1950s.[2] They were later joined by an unknown number of Iraqi emigrants from Israel.

The Israeli government, which chose to block the return of the Palestinian refugees, was now quicker and more explicit in establishing a link between the rights of the Palestinian refugees and the rights of the Iraqi Jews. A few days after the Iraqi government issued regulations No 3 of 1951 in freezing the property of Jews deprived of Iraqi nationality, Moshe Sharett, the Israeli Foreign Minister at the time announced:

---

1. Most of these people left Iraq in the early 1960s after the collapse of the Qasim regime, which was considered among the most tolerant towards the Jews. In fact, a few hundred Jews had returned to Iraq during his rule, but more left in the late 1960s and early 1970s.

2. The American report of March 1949 put the total number of Iraqi Jews at 180,000. The Shaul Sasson report of December 1950 put the number at 150,000. Assuming that 140,000 is a more realistic estimate, and that the number of those who arrived in Israel was 125,000, then about 10,000–15,000 Jews settled outside Israel.

An account already exists between us and the Arab world: the account of the compensation that accrues to the Arabs who left the territory of Israel and abandoned their property … The act that has now been perpetrated by the kingdom of Iraq … forces us to link the two the two accounts … We will take into account the value of the Jewish property that has been frozen in Iraq when calculating the compensation that have that we have undertaken to pay the Arabs who abandoned property in Israel.[1]

Drawing on Israeli archival sources, Yehouda Shenhav, (1999) noticed that the Israeli government turned this link into 'a system akin to double-entry accounting with regard to the two sets of property – that of the 1948 Palestinian refugees and of the Iraqi Jews – thereby neutralising the claims of both'.[2] In his view, the Israeli government cited the injustice that the Iraqi government had done the Jews of Iraq to explain its refusal to compensate the Palestinians, but told the Iraqi Jews in Israel to apply so that the same Iraqi government could bring about restitution. Shenhav sees that this accounting logic was not necessarily a pre-planned scheme by the Israeli government but rather 'by exploiting circumstances' which it actually created. He acknowledges that when implemented as *raison d'état*, 'it enabled the Israeli government to absolve itself of responsibility for compensating both the Iraqi Jews and the Palestinian refugees'.[3]

A new World Organization of Jews from the Arab Countries (WOJAC) was established in Israel in 1975. It was led by Mordechai Ben-Porat , the former Zionist leader in Iraq who was behind the bombs in Baghdad and later became a member of Moshe Dayan's Rafi party, and cabinet minister, who argued that Palestinian refugees

---

1. Quoted by Shenhav, Yehouda (1999): 'The Jews of Iraq, Zionist Ideology, and the Property of the Palestinian Refugees of 1948: An Anomaly of National Accounting', *International Journal of Middle East Studies*, no. 31,Cambridge University Press, pp. 605–30.
2. Ibid., p. 606.
3. Ibid., p. 606.

should not be allowed back into Israel, since an involuntary population exchange had already taken place in the Middle East. The organization adopted a resolution casting responsibility on the Arab governments. Speaking at the UN General Assembly in December 1977, Ben-Porat stated that 'the problem of the Arab and Jewish refugees in the Middle East can find its practical solution only within the framework of de facto exchanges of population which have already taken place.'[1] WOJAC, too, held that they should be used to enhance the bargaining power of the Israeli government, not to support individual claims. Shenhav clearly sees that the Israeli government has used the population exchange argument to deny the rights of the Palestinians to return to Palestine or to claim compensation for their 'lost' property.[2]

1. Ibid., p. 622.
2. Ibid., p. 622.

Conclusion

The mass emigration of Iraqi Jews was made possible by Law 1/1950, but must be understood in the light of developments following the establishment of Israel in May 1948. Before then, Jewish emigration from Iraq was only on a small scale and the emigrants did not necessarily settle in Palestine. In the main, this emigration was not the result of Zionist influence or of ill-treatment of Jews in Iraq.

Push factors, whether latent or active, seem to have played a smaller role in the case of Iraqi Jews compared with Jews of other Arab countries for, as we saw in chapters 1–3, the Iraqis were more closely integrated into the society in which they lived. Their identification with ruling authorities, however, may explain the one significant large-scale act of violence against them (the Farhud).

Palestine, and later Israel, did not constitute a significant ideological or economic pull factor for Iraqi Jews, who, like other oriental Jews, were generally sceptical or antagonistic to Zionism.

The establishment of the state of Israel had a significant effect on the position of Iraqi Jews. Its consequences were probably more dramatic for them than for any other Jewish community in the Arab world. The war in Palestine stemmed the rise of the national opposition movement. The consensus that democratic reforms were the priority collapsed, and the difference between Judaism and Zionism became blurred for some nationalist forces. The war gave the authorities an opportunity to emerge from their internal crisis and to use martial law to impose on Jews restrictions that implied that they were to be regarded with suspicion.

The stance of the authorities and of some extreme nationalists, however, should not be construed as a radical change in the attitude of Iraqi society as a whole toward the Jews. Persecution of Jews took place within a much broader campaign by the authorities (using martial law) against democratic forces. Anti-Jewish measures were temporary, and their severity seems to have fluctuated depending on the prospects of peace in Palestine. The anxiety felt by Iraqi Jews likewise seems to have varied with peace prospects in Palestine. The war and the establishment of Israel therefore do not provide sufficient explanation for the exodus.

Israel's need for labour power and its wider political interest in population exchanges were well served by the transfer schemes proposed by the British authorities. The denaturalization law and the freezing of their property may have been influenced by such British suggestions and more crucially as a reaction of well organised and effective world-wide Zionist campaign to bring the Iraqi Jews to Israel and to link and thereby neutralise the claims of both the Palestinian refugees and the Iraqi Jews. There is no evidence, however, that the exodus came as a result of a secret official agreement between both Iraqi and the Israeli governments. Nor did the Iraqi government foresee the scale of the emigration that followed. In fact neither government was interested in an official deal; such a formula would bring too much embarrassment for the Iraqi government to bear, while there is now more evidence to suggest that despite the Israeli government's efforts to bring the Iraqi Jews to Israel, it was more convenient and less costly for the Israeli government not to enter into an official deal with the Iraqi government. By so doing, the Israeli government effectively annulled the rights of both Palestinian refugees and Iraqi Jews.

Neither the Iraqi government nor the leadership of the Jewish community succeeded in reducing the anxiety felt by the Jewish community about prospects in Iraq, anxiety that was exploited by the Zionist movement. Two series of events were of special significance in the crucial period following the promulgation of the law: the Hillel-Suwaidi agreement on evacuation arrangements and the bomb attacks organized by Zionist agents. The evacuation agreement legitimated the Zionists' position (and introduced a hitherto insignificant American interest), while the second 'helped many Jews to make up their minds'.

Law No. 1 of 1950

FO 371/82478 Dispatch No. 55 (1571/8/50)

Annexure to the Ordinance for the Cancellation of Iraqi Nationality (Law No. 62 of 1933).

Passed by the Iraqi Chamber of Deputies on 2 March 1950 and by the Iraqi Senate on 4 March 1950, as Law No. 1 of 1950.

Enclosure no. 1 in Sir Henry B. Mack's confidential dispatch no. 55.

Article 1
The Council of Ministers is empowered to divest any Iraqi Jew who, of his own free will and choice, desires to leave Iraq for good of his Iraqi nationality after he has signed a special form in the presence of an official appointed by the Minister of the Interior.

Article 2
Any Iraqi Jew who leaves Iraq or tries to leave Iraq illegally will forfeit his Iraqi nationality by decision of the Council of Ministers.

Article 3
Any Iraqi Jew who has already left Iraq illegally will be considered to have left Iraq for good if he does not return within a period of two months from the date of the putting into operation of this law, and he will lose his Iraqi nationality at the end of that period.

Article 4
The Minister of the Interior must order the deportation of anyone who has lost Iraqi nationality under Articles 1 and 2 unless the Minister is convinced by sufficient reasons that his temporary stay in Iraq is necessary for judicial or legal reasons, or to safeguard someone else's officially testified rights.

Article 5
This law will remain in force for a period of one year from the date of its coming into effect and may be cancelled at any time during that period by a Royal Iradah published in the *Official Gazette*.

Article 6
This law comes into force from the date of its publication in the *Official Gazette*.

Article 7
The Minister of the Interior will execute this law.

Supporting Arguments
It has been noticed that some Iraqi Jews are attempting by every illegal means to leave Iraq for good and that others have already left Iraq illegally. As the presence of subjects of this description forced to stay in the country and obliged to keep their Iraqi nationality would inevitably lead to results affecting public security and give rise to social and economic problems, it has been found advisable not to prevent those wishing to do so from leaving Iraq for good, forfeiting their Iraqi nationality. This law has been promulgated to this end.

Report by the US Embassy in Baghdad on Emigration of the Iraqi Jewish Community

FO 371/75182, E 397/1571/93

Airgram

SECRET

Secretary of State   Baghdad
Washington   March 8, 1949

The following are the Embassy's views concerning the four questions posed in the Department's Circular Airgram dated Feb. 7, 1949, 8:50 a.m. regarding the Jewish community in Iraq:

1. What attitude would be adopted by the Iraqi government towards the emigration of its Jewish community?

   A few extreme nationalists have from time to time put forward the idea that Iraq should get rid of all of its Jews. However, any government which Iraq is likely to have in the foreseeable future would be reluctant to permit the emigration of the Jewish community. Responsible leaders recognize the fact that a mass exodus of the Jews, who play such a prominent role in financial and business circles in Iraq, would seriously disrupt the economy of the country, further endangering its precarious stability.

2. What would be the general attitude of the Jewish community towards the possibility of emigration?

The question is practically impossible to answer on any verifiable basis without undertaking a detailed survey of opinion among the various income groups, age groups, attitude groups (e.g. Europeanized versus orientals), occupational groups, et cetera, of which the Jewish community is composed.

The Embassy's rough estimates as to what the attitudes of the Jewish community towards the possibility of emigration to Palestine may be are as follows:

1. Older non-Europeanized religious leaders, rabbis and their followers, would not at present, or in the foreseeable future, want to give up their established positions here in exchange for an unpredictable fate in Palestine.
2. Leaders of the Jewish financial and business community, who are to a large extent Europeanized, would probably be divided on the question: a) those who have emotionally identified themselves with the Zionist state, or who have exaggerated fears of possible future Iraqi action against them, would want to go to Palestine, even if considerable sacrifice is involved; b) those who have not identified themselves with the Zionist state and regard themselves as Iraqis (perhaps the majority) would probably prefer maintaining their present comparatively comfortable and economically privileged positions in Iraq, to embarking on an uncertain future in Israel.
3. Many younger men, of the 'white collar' class, roughly those aged 30 and younger, who are not yet firmly established in their economic activities, would be interested in emigrating to Israel, in the belief that they would have better opportunities there than in Iraq.
4. Many of the several hundred officials discharged from service in the Iraqi Government, or such organizations as the Basra Port Authority and the Iraq Petroleum Company, as a result of Iraq's being at war with the Jews in Palestine, would like to emigrate to Israel.
5. Small tradesmen, artisans, etc., are unlikely to be interested in emigration to Israel, unless the community's religious and economic leaders (whose attitudes are estimated above) make active propaganda to persuade them.

All of the above estimates are made on the assumption that active warfare in Palestine is coming to a stop, and some sort of settlement along the lines of the UN General Assembly resolution of December 11, 1948 will be effected. The Iraqi Government's attitude under the Pachachi cabinet and the present Nuri al-Said cabinet toward the Jewish community has on the whole been reasonable and moderate. Muzaham Pachachi's words on the subject at the time of his controversy with Sadiq Bassam in September 1948 (Ambtel 585, Sept. 29, 1948) are worth recalling: 'Jews are Iraqi nationals, and there is no policy against them. If Bassam thinks martial law was proclaimed in the ??? to tyrannize and combat Jews, we disagree. If this controversy with us is over this policy, we say proudly that we oppose him because tyranny has never been an instrument of sound statesmanship.'

The Iraqis fear that Israel may attempt by aggressive action to expand its present boundaries. If this occurs, Iraqi attitude toward the Jewish community and the treatment of Jews would change severely for the worse, inducing a greater proportion of Iraqi Jews to want to leave Iraq and face the risks and uncertainties of emigration to Israel.

In other words, the desire of the Jewish community to emigrate will in great part be induced or limited by the amount of aggressiveness and recalcitrance which Israel may display in the future. To the degree that stability in Palestine and the Middle East is disturbed by Israel's pursuance of a policy of expansionism, the Iraqi Jews will suffer more disabilities; the community as a whole might eventually come to welcome the possibility of emigration. If Israel, however, pursues a policy of moderation and agrees to a peace settlement considered not too unreasonable by the Arabs, not more than a small proportion of Iraq's Jewish community would want to emigrate to Palestine.

3. What would be the economic effects on Iraq if the Jewish community should emigrate?

    How severe the resultant economic effect would be if the Jewish community were to emigrate is debatable. However, basic factors which should be borne in mind in attempting to form an opinion are the following:

1. Possible effect on the import trade:

   A high proportion (estimated at 75 per cent) of Iraq's import trade is in the hands of Jewish firms. For a number of years at least, chaotic conditions in this branch of Iraq's economy would result if these firms should disappear rapidly. Only a small number of Moslem Iraqis have sufficient capital, requisite financial skill, and willingness to make heavy comparatively long-term investments of the type required in the import business in Iraq, to fill the vacuum that would be left should the Jewish community leave.

2. Possible effect on the export trade:

   In the case of the export trade, the effect would probably be less, since the major portion of this trade, which is largely in agricultural products, is in Arab and foreign hands.

3. Internal distribution of imported goods:

   The internal distribution of imported goods might break down to a dangerous extent, since a high proportion (estimated at 50 per cent) of importers, wholesalers, and shopkeepers dealing in imported goods are Jews.

4. Possible effect on the financing of small-scale business:

   A high percentage of internal trade in Iraq is carried on with the help of 'Sarrafs' (money-lenders) most of whom are Jews, who supply the working capital for small businesses, shopkeepers, dealers in agricultural products, etc. Should the Jewish 'Sarrafs' leave Iraq, much of the country's business of these types might well be disrupted.

5. Possible effect on real-estate and land values in Baghdad:

   A high proportion of Baghdad's more modern residential dwellings and business buildings are owned by Jews. Should the Jews start disposing of these buildings under distressed sales conditions, the bottom might well drop out of the real-estate market in Baghdad.

6. Possible effect of emigration of Jewish clerical 'white collar' class:

> Until the outbreak of hostilities in Palestine many Moslems considered Jews ideally suited for clerical work, and their presence was considered indispensable for the smooth functioning of the machinery. Clerical staffs in banks, commercial organizations, and oil companies were primarily recruited from Jewish ranks.
>
> Since May 15, a considerable number of these people have been dismissed and replaced by Christian and Moslem clerks (in that order). Their efficiency, especially that of the Moslems, is far below that of the Jews.
>
> However, a considerable number of Jewish clerks are still employed in Jewish and non-Jewish business firms, and if all of them leave for Palestine, the efficiency of many Iraqi business organizations would deteriorate.

To sum up, Iraq's economy would suffer if it lost its Jewish community, the business leaders of which are the most adaptable, intelligent, and progressive group in the entire Iraq economy. How severe the effect would be is difficult to predict, but it seems clear that, should the community emigrate, (a) the importation of processed goods might be for a number of years seriously disrupted, with many consequences which might seriously endanger the country's stability, (b) the export trade would suffer to a lesser extent, (c) the internal distribution of imported goods would be disrupted, (d) many small businesses would have great difficulty in financing their operations, (e) land values in Baghdad would fall sharply, and (f) the loss of the Jewish clerical 'white collar' employees would adversely affect the operations of many important Moslem and foreign firms.

All of these factors taken together might well have a serious adverse effect not only on the economy, but also on the internal stability and security of Iraq.

4. Current estimate of the size of the Jewish community:

No official population statistics have been published (or made otherwise available) for many years. The Embassy's current rough estimate is as follows:

Urban Jews:	120,000 (perhaps 90,000 in Baghdad and 30,000 in other towns)
Rural Jews (who are more or less completely assimilated Iraqis and perhaps should not be considered as members of the Jewish community within the frame of reference of this report):	60,000
Total	180,000

F.O. Summary of Correspondence with British Legations, Autumn 1949, on Proposed Exchange of Iraqi Jews for Arab Refugees

FO 371/75152, E 13371

On 5th September we asked Baghdad, British Middle East Office, Jerusalem, and Tel Aviv for their views on the desirability of encouraging an arrangement whereby the Iraqi Jews would be moved into Israel, receiving compensation for their property from the Israel Government, while a broadly equivalent number of Arab refugees would be installed … in Iraq. The replies of these posts have now been received. The consensus of opinion seems against encouraging the exchange of Iraqi Jews for Arab refugees from Palestine, though it is recognized that such a scheme would have some advantages.

The main points which have been made are:

(1) Difficulties in arranging compensation. Tel Aviv says that Israel is unlikely to compensate Iraqi Jews in the present state of the national finances, and it is unlikely that Iraq would allow them to take their property with them.

(2) 'Exchange' might quickly deteriorate into expulsion of Iraqi Jews. Reports are already current of persecution of Iraqi Jews and His Majesty's Government does not want to be held responsible for a pogrom. Moreover, anti-Jew measures might spread to other states in the Middle East. Baghdad points out in addition that by suggesting exchange we should be admitting that the Iraqi Jews have no right to be in Iraq.

(3) Economically Israel does not need the townsmen who constitute the majority of Iraqi Jews, especially if they were forced to come

without their capital. Nevertheless, Tel Aviv thinks that Israel would probably receive any Iraqi Jews who desired to immigrate.

(4) Indeed, Tel Aviv believes that unless persecution develops, the Iraqi Jews are probably better off in Iraq than they would be in Israel. Jerusalem says that Israel would care little for their hardships, which the Iraqi Jews might suffer by the transfer, and that they would exploit the situation to blame His Majesty's Government for their hardships.

(5) Baghdad points out that Iraq is not particularly keen to welcome Arab refugees in any case: and those who come might not fill the gaps in the Iraqi economy left by the departing Jews. In fact, since the Palestine Arabs are mostly cultivators and Iraqi Jews mostly townsmen, the exchange might be economically unsound from the point of view of both parties.

(6) Militarily and economically Israel might like to keep nests of Jews in the Arab states, especially if it intends, as BMEO suggests, to embark on a policy of 'economic integration' in the Middle East.

(7) The elimination of certain minorities might lead to more stability and better relations in the Middle East. BMEO points to the Greco-Turkish exchange of population as an example. But it might, even so, have the opposite effect of increasing national exuberance.

The economic arguments against the exchange of Iraqi Jews for Arab refugees are strong. Iraq, Israel, and Iraqi Jews will probably all lose by the transaction. The only gainers will be the Arab refugees. I believe however that a good deal of the anticipated economic and social difficulties could be overcome if the exchange were supervised by an international commission. If the exchange were agreed between Iraq and Israel, they might both welcome the assistance of such a commission.

Political arguments all seem to me to be in favour of the exchange. The major arguments are:

(a) the Israel Government is most unlikely to be able to refuse to accept Iraqi Jews even if it wanted to. Our influence in Tel Aviv is probably strong enough to prevent the exploiting of the situation to blame His Majesty's Government for hardships (paragraph (4) above);

(b) the inability of the Israel Government to refuse to accept Jews should be used to prevent its using the Iraqi Jews to further the policy of 'economic integration' of the Middle East under Israel hegemony (paragraph (6) above);

(c) 'national exuberance' is a phenomenon which is going to last a long time in the Middle East. On the whole, the elimination of awkward minorities is likely to cool rather than fan the flames. The present situation in which charges of sedition against Iraqi Jews are likely to be well founded may at any time result in Israel charges that Iraqi Jews are being persecuted, at least by the mob, having equal foundation. I can think of nothing more calculated to disturb the process of reconciliation between Israel and the Arabs.

Conclusion

Nothing should be done to discourage an amicable arrangement between Iraq and Israel leading to the exchange of Arab refugees for Iraqi Jews. We should not, however, press either the Iraqis or Israelis to initiate action and if questioned should say that this is a matter which should be left to the governments concerned.

J.G.T. Sheringham

I agree with Mr Sheringham that the essence of the scheme is prior agreement between Iraq and Israel and that until such agreement is reached we should be well advised to steer clear.

A.M. Williams

British View of Denaturalization Bill

FO 371/82478, EQ 1571/8

Confidential   British Embassy
No. 55   Baghdad
1571/8/50   7 March, 1950

Sir,

1. In my telegram no. 117 of the 3rd March, I reported that the Iraq Government had secured the passage through the Lower House of a Bill which empowers the Council of Ministers to deprive an Iraqi Jew who wishes of his own free will and choice to leave Iraq for good, of his Iraqi nationality. I now have the honour to transmit a copy in translation of this Bill, which was passed by the Senate on March 4th and awaits Royal assent.

2. The Prime Minister informed me after dinner on February 25th that the Cabinet were drafting a law of this kind. He himself had wished to make no mention of the Jews, but the Minister of Interior had said that this was essential. I asked the Prime Minister how many would be involved and if it was not possible to let them go by the issue of an administrative order. He said that he thought about 6 or 7,000 would go and the Minister of Interior considered that a law was necessary. I said I had always been in favour of those Jews who wished to leave the country being allowed to go. Any law, however, would have to be very carefully drafted and the Iraq Government must be careful not to

include anything in it which could be represented as anti-Semitic. The Prime Minister asked me to let him know my considered views as soon as I had had time to study the question.

3. I had arranged accordingly to see the Prime Minister on March 2nd and was intending to make the following points to him:
   (1) Any law dealing with the Iraqi Jewish community is certain to be widely publicized in the world press.
   (2) If its provisions can be represented as harsh or discriminatory the Iraqi Government will be the object of strong attacks, and they should therefore consider carefully what their reply would be.
   (3) The Iraqi Government should find out whether and under what conditions the Egyptian and Lebanese Governments have permitted their Jewish citizens to leave for Israel. If they can quote a precedent action taken in other Arab states which has not been the subject of criticism, their position will be stronger.
   (4) The Iraqi Government should study the action taken by the Israeli Government in respect of the property left behind by the Arab refugees.
   (5) The Iraqi Government's position before world opinion would be very much stronger if they lifted restrictions at the same time on those Jews who were willing to stay in Iraq, and could therefore announce that there were no legal or administrative restrictions on Iraqi Jews which did not apply to all Iraqi citizens.

4. The United States Ambassador was also consulted by the Prime Minister but he declined to put forward any views. He told me, however, that he personally agreed with the points which I was proposing to make to the Prime Minister.

5. In the event I did not see the Prime Minister, who was busy in Parliament, until March 4th, by which time the draft law had already passed the Lower House. When I saw him, I reminded him of our conversation of the 22nd February and I informed him of what I would have said to him if I had had an opportunity of seeing him before the law had been presented to Parliament. He thanked me and said that the Iraq Government had decided to deal with the question gradually. They had therefore dealt with the departure of the Jews as an amendment to the Nationality Law and had decided not to define at this stage the amount of money which Jews who wished to leave were to be allowed

to take with them. They had first thought of making it ID100. Those who left would, however, want to take pounds sterling with them. The amount they would be allowed to take depended, therefore, on the number who decided to go. It was impossible to tell at present what the number would be. When this was known a decision would be taken. He thought that they might be allowed to take from ID50 to ID70. All those who would want to go were poor. On the question of property he was glad to be able to tell me that there was now no restriction on the transfer of property by Jews inside Iraq. The restriction had been lifted four days ago by an administrative order issued by the Minister of Justice. There were therefore no restrictions left on Iraqi Jews which did not apply to all Iraqi citizens. The Prime Minister said that both Jews and Moslems were pleased with the law. The Jews felt that the departure of the malcontents would facilitate good treatment for the remainder. He said that the Jews who left would not be 'stateless' since they would be given a laissez passer on leaving. He presumably meant by this only that they would carry a proof of their origin.

6. The law was introduced as an annexure to the Ordinance for the Cancellation of Iraqi Nationality (Law No. 62 of 1933). It was attacked in the Chamber by the Independence [Istiqlal] Party on the grounds that it did not provide a radical solution to the problem. There was also criticism from other opposition elements of the emergency procedure adopted by the Government in debating this law.

7. Among the 'reasons in support of the law' attached to the draft law as presented to the House is the statement that Jews have been resorting to illegitimate means to leave Iraq and that others have already left Iraq illegitimately. This exodus has been taking place at an increasing rate since the lifting of martial law in December 1949. (It was quoted to me by the Prime Minister as one of the reasons for speedy action.) Under martial law, attempts by Jews to leave Iraq illegally could be severely punished under such charges as 'attempting to join Zionist bands in Palestine'. Since the lifting of martial law, illegal departure from Iraq could only be dealt with under the passport law (No. 65 of 1932), the offender being liable to the maximum penalty of six months imprisonment or a fine of ID100.

8. The numbers involved in this illegal movement can only be guessed at. According to the Mutasarrif of Basra, through whose liwa most of them

passed, the traffic into Persia probably amounted to 30 or 40 persons a day. The successful emigrants went to Tehran, where aircraft were chartered specially to take parties to Israel without touching down in Arab countries. Funds had been accumulated by Jews in Persia who persuaded Persian Moslem pilgrims to Kerbala and Nejef to take sight drafts on merchants in Baghdad for their expenses in Iraq. Money was also being smuggled out by illicit Jewish emigrants. The Mutasarrif told the Consul-General that he had protested to the Ministry of Interior that the present regulations, that is, prior to this new law, were undermining all administration in Basra liwa because the bribes available were so heavy and so tempting.

9. The reasons for the desire of many Jews to leave Iraq are, I think, apparent from my despatch No. 236 of the 12th December 1949. Although the Prime Minister has said that all administrative restrictions on Jews are now abolished, the disabilities under which they suffered were practical rather than administrative and these may well continue. Examples of these disabilities are that Jews were, in practice, largely debarred from official employment; new Jewish entrants to the professions could seldom obtain licences to practise; opportunities for commercial enterprise for Jews were restricted and there was the constant fear that the re-imposition of martial law might again expose the Jewish community to the injustices which they had suffered during 1948–49.

10. As far as I can judge at present, the Prime Minister's view that both Jews and Moslems are pleased with the new law is correct, although Arab Nationalists criticize its provisions as being too favourable to the Jews, while there is apprehension among some Jews about what will happen to their property or to their families who may be left behind.

> I have the honour to be,
> With the highest respect,
> Sir,
> Your most obedient
>   humble servant
> Humphrey Trevelyan

Documents on Control and Administration of Property of Jews Deprived of Iraqi Nationality

5A
Law No. 5 of 1951: Control and Administration of Property of Jews Deprived of Iraqi Nationality

FO 371/91690, EQ 1571/30

Translated from *al-Waqayi al-Iraqiyah*, no. 2938 dated 10 March 1951.

Enclosure in confidential despatch no. 44 (1572/36/51), Baghdad to London, 14 March 1951.

In accordance with Article 23 (as amended) of the Organic Law, with the approval of the Senate and the Chamber of Deputies, and by virtue of the rights vested in us, we hereby order the enactment of the following Law on behalf of His Royal Highness the Regent.

Article 1
The following expressions shall have the meanings indicated against each:
   The Minister: Minister of Interior.
   The Custodian General: The person to be appointed by a decision of the Council of Ministers to undertake the duties determined by this Law and the Regulations to be issued thereunder.
   Person who has been deprived of his Iraqi nationality: Every Iraqi who has been deprived of his Iraqi nationality in accordance with Law No. 1 of 1950.

Property: Consists of immovable property belonging to the denationalized person, or the immovable property which is in his possession in any form of insurance, rent, mortgage or any other form and the proceeds of the sale of such immovable property, its value as mortgage, insurance, lease and development, and the rights pertaining thereto, and also deposits, debts, cash, currencies, stocks, bills of lading, drafts, negotiable bills, and any claims due to him in cash or in kind.

Article 2

(a) The property of persons who have been deprived of Iraqi nationality shall be frozen and shall not be disposed of in any way whatsoever with effect from the date of the coming into force of this law. Disposal of such property will be in accordance with the provisions of this law and the regulations to be issued thereunder.

(b) The Office of the Custodian General for the Control and Administration of the Property of Denationalized Persons will be established under the presidency of the Custodian General in accordance with a cadre to be determined by the Council of Ministers. The salaries of the officials of this Office and the necessary expenses incurred in accordance with this law and the regulations to be issued thereunder will be met from the property at the disposal of the Custodian General.

Article 3

Regulations for the purpose of the execution of this law will be issued on the following matters:

(a) The authority and powers of the Custodian General, and the manner of the administration, safeguarding, disposal, freezing and liquidation of the property.

(b) The obligations in regard to the disposal of property belonging to denationalized persons devolving upon real and juristic persons, and interested persons, governmental and quasi-governmental departments and officials.

Article 4

The transactions and contracts carried out by the Custodian General and the decisions issued by him in accordance with this law and the regulations to be issued thereunder will be valid.

Article 5

(a) Any person contravening the provisions of this law and the regulations issued thereunder or the orders and instructions issued thereunder will be punished by imprisonment for a period not exceeding 2 years or by a fine not exceeding ID4,000, or by both.

(b) The penalties provided for under this law do not preclude proceedings against a person contravening this law for the damages resulting from losses caused by his contraventions, and the Custodian General or his representative may file a suit and claim damages from such a person either in connection with the criminal suit which has been filed or otherwise from the competent court.

Article 6

After the coming into force of this law, the disposal by any person, other than the Custodian General, of property belonging to a denationalized person shall not be valid, and any such disposal shall be null and void.

Article 7

Any interested party who considers himself aggrieved by the decisions of the Custodian General may appeal to the Minister against the decision of the Custodian General within one month from the date of issue of the decision. The decision of the Minister shall be final.

Article 8

This law shall come into force from the date of its publication in the *Official Gazette*.

Article 9

The Ministers of State are charged with the execution of this law.
Done at Baghdad this 2nd day of Jamad al-Thani 1370 and the 10th day of March 1951.

Regency Council: JAMIL AL-MADFAI
                                    HUSSAIN BIN ALI
                                    MUHAMMAD AL-SADR
                                    (All Ministers)

5B
Regulation No. 3 of 1951: Control and Administration of Property of Jews Deprived of Iraqi Nationality

FO 371/91690, EQ 1571/30

Translated from *al-Waqayi al-Iraqiyah*, no. 2939 dated 10 March 1951.

Enclosure in a confidential despatch no. 44E 1572/36/51, Baghdad to London, 14th March 1951.

After reference to Article 3 of the law for the Control and Administration of Property of Jews who have been deprived of Iraqi Nationality No. 5 of 1951, by virtue of the powers vested in us under Article 23 (Amended) of the Organic Law, and with the approval of the Council of Ministers, we hereby order the enactment of the following Regulation on behalf of His Royal Highness the Regent.

Article 1
The Custodian General may exercise the following powers:
(a) To sequester, administer, dispose of, and liquidate all property belonging to a de-naturalized person in accordance with the provisions of the said law and of this Regulation.
(b) To represent a de-naturalized person before the Courts and government departments, etc., or appoint an agent to represent him before the Courts, government departments, etc.
(c) To appoint custodians to administer the property of de-naturalized persons.
(d) To liquidate the business or commercial premises belonging to a de-naturalized person, appoint custodians for this purpose, and pay the salaries and expenses required therefor.
(e) To sign all transactions required for the administration, liquidation or freezing of property in accordance with the provisions of this law.
(f) To replace a de-naturalized person in companies continuing in operation or in companies which he finds no justification to dissolve, or to depute someone else for this purpose, also to exercise all the rights of a de-naturalized person in accordance with this regulation.
(g) To take delivery of property, bills of lading and documents belonging to a de-naturalized person and to dispose of them in accordance with the provisions of this Regulation.

(h) To pay the Shara (legal) maintenance allowance imposed by the competent courts to persons maintained by a de-naturalized person from his property, if such persons have no one to support them or have no means of livelihood, and also to pay from his property the passage expenses of a de-naturalized person and persons maintained by him and their maintenance expenses until their expatriation.

(i) To inspect the books, entries and documents belonging to any juristic or real person who, in the reasonable belief of the Custodian General, possesses or has at his disposal property belonging to a de-naturalized person, or to depute some other person to undertake this inspection.

(j) Any other measures or powers which the Council of Ministers may, from time to time, decide to delegate to the Custodian General for the purpose of this Regulation.

Article 2

The Custodian General may sell the immovable property belonging to a de-naturalized person in the following circumstances:

(a) To discharge the obligations due from him to the Treasury, government departments, the Water and Electricity Board, Municipalities and all quasi-governmental departments.

(b) To redeem established debts due from him, in accordance with a decree which has acquired finality, based on a document authenticated by the Notary Public before the coming into force of Law No. 5 of 1951, or to liquidate a mortgage or insurance transaction supported by a Tapu Sanad issued before the coming into force of this Regulation.

(c) If the property is in such condition that it is about to collapse or cannot be utilized.

(d) To pay the maintenance allowance due from him in accordance with the provisions of paragraph (h) of the preceding article.

(e) To pay any expenses or charges in accordance with this Regulation.

Article 3

If the Custodian General is convinced that the continuance of the company established by a de-naturalized person, or of the company in which he is a shareholder, is harmful; or would lead to the smuggling of goods from Iraq; or would contravene the provisions of Law No. 5 of 1951 and of this Regulation; or that a legal justification exists; he may demand the dissolution and liquidation of the company and may also dispose of the shares in accordance with the provisions of law.

Article 4

Subject to the provisions of Article 2, the Custodian General should freeze all the property belonging to a de-naturalized person and should prevent the export from Iraq of any part thereof. He should also forbid any transaction in connection with such goods other than for the purposes indicated in this Regulation.

Article 5

All Sarrafs, banks, real or juristic persons, government and quasi-governmental departments should comply with the following:

(a) Any person who has in his possession or at his disposal immovable property belonging to a de-naturalized person, if he disposes of such property as an agent, or holds it in trust or on loan, should refrain from disposing of it by any means, and should submit to the Custodian General, within 20 days from the date of coming into force of this Regulation, a statement elucidating the nature, particulars, number, locality and Tapu Sanads, if any, of such property and give a written undertaking that he will not dispose of such property.

(b) If the immovable property is in the possession of a person by virtue of partnership, mortgage, insurance or lease, he should refrain from carrying out any transaction in connection with it, should submit the statement indicated in the preceding paragraph within the period stipulated therein, should submit the explanations required from him by the Custodian General and should carry out the instructions issued by the Custodian General as to the manner of disposal of such property.

(c) Any Sarraf and any person who has in his possession Iraqi or foreign coins, or currency, deposits, bonds, negotiable bills, stocks or any other property, other than immovable property, belonging to a de-naturalized person, should refrain from carrying out any transaction in connection with them or from letting them out of his possession in any way whatsoever. He should hand over such property, within 15 days from the date of coming into force of this Regulation, to the Custodian General and should submit the details which the Custodian General may require from him.

(d) Any bank which has in its possession Iraqi or foreign coins, or currency, deposits, bonds, stocks or any property belonging to a de-naturalized person, should refrain from disposing of such property or carrying out any transaction in connection with it from the date of coming into force of this Regulation. The bank should submit to the Custodian General, within 15 days from the date of coming into force of this Regulation, a statement embodying the nature, particulars and amount of such property, together with any observations the bank may have. The bank should retain such property and dispose of it in accordance with instructions which it will receive from the Custodian General.

(e) From the date of coming into force of this Regulation, Tapu Departments should refrain from carrying out any transaction relating to a de-naturalized person in respect of immovable property belonging to him or which is in his possession, unless such Departments receive an order from the Custodian General. Tapu Departments should dispose of such property in accordance with decisions to be taken.

(f) The Departments of Customs and Excise, Imports, and other governmental and quasi-governmental departments should forward to the Custodian General all property, bills of lading and other commercial documents belonging to a de-naturalized person within 10 days, and should not carry out any transaction in connection with such documents nor dispose of them from the date of coming into force of this Regulation. Such goods will be disposed of according to instructions to be issued by the Custodian General.

Article 6
This Regulation shall come into force from the date of its publication in the *Official Gazette*.

Article 7
The Ministers of State are charged with the execution of this Regulation. Done at Baghdad this 2nd day of Jamad al-Thani 1370 and the 10th day of March 1951.

Regency Council: JAMIL AL-MADFAI
                                                 HUSSAIN BIN ALI
                                                MUHAMMAD AL-SADR
                                                (All Ministers)

5C
Law No. 12 of 1951, Supplemental to Law No. 5 of 1951: Control and Administration of Property of Jews Who Have Renounced Iraqi Nationality

FO 371/91690, EQ 1571/46

Translated from *al-Waqayi al-Iraqiyah*, no. 2949 dated 22 March 1951.

With the approval of the Senate and the Chamber of Deputies, We hereby order the enactment of the following Law:

Article 1
With effect from the date of coming into force of this Law, the property of Iraqi Jews who left Iraq with a passport with effect from the 1st day of the year 1948 shall be frozen, and the provisions of Law No. 5 of 1951 and the Regulations which have been issued, or which may be issued, thereunder shall apply thereto.

Article 2
(a) Any Iraqi Jew covered by Article 1 must return to Iraq within 2 months from the date of the notification to be issued under the terms of the following paragraph.
(b) Iraqi Diplomatic and Consular Missions in Foreign Countries and Diplomatic and Consular Missions in Foreign Countries in charge of Iraqi interests should publish a notification in a newspaper in the capital of the country requiring the persons covered by the provisions of the preceding paragraph to return to Iraq within 2 months from the date of the publication of such notification.
(c) Any person covered by the provisions of the preceding paragraph who does not return to Iraq within the period indicated in the notification will be considered as having left Iraq finally and shall forfeit his Iraqi nationality with effect from the date of termination of that period, and the provisions of Law No. 5 of 1951 and the Regulations which have been issued, or which may be issued, thereunder will apply to him.
(d) If he returns to Iraq before the termination of the period stipulated, his frozen property will be restored to him after the deduction of such administrative charges as will be determined by the Custodian General and of the expenses incurred by him for the execution of the Law.

Article 3

(a) There shall be excluded from the provisions of paragraph (c) of Article 2 those who prove, during the period provided for therein, that their remaining outside Iraq is based on one of the following reasons:

(i) If he were sick in a hospital or was looking after one of his relatives (up to and including the third degree) or his wife who was ill and the illness prevented him from travelling, provided that this is confirmed by a medical certificate issued by a recognized authority.

(ii) If he were engaged in studies and had not completed his 27th year provided that this is confirmed by a certificate from a recognized scholastic institute.

(b) Certificates confirming the two reasons indicated in the preceding paragraph should be accompanied by a document issued by Iraqi Diplomatic or Consular Missions or those in charge of Iraqi interests in a foreign country confirming the facts of the case together with a testimony of one of its members or officials deputed by it to witness the fact.

(c) If the reason for which those who failed to return ceased to exist during the period of 2 months and they do not return to Iraq within one month from the date of its ceasing to exist, they will be considered to have left Iraq finally and shall forfeit their Iraqi nationality and the provisions of Law No. 5 of 1951 and the Regulations which have been issued, or which may be issued, thereunder shall apply to them.

Article 4

(i) The provisions of the original law and the Regulations which have been issued, or which may be issued, thereunder and the provisions of this Law shall apply to any Iraqi Jew who left Iraq with a passport before the 1st day of the year 1948 and his property shall be frozen in the following circumstances:

(a) If he had not usually resided in a foreign country, or if he usually resided in a foreign country and the government considers that there are reasons requiring that he should return to Iraq.

(b) If the Custodian General is not convinced that he had an established business in a foreign country before the above-mentioned date and had a branch in Iraq undertaking commercial business, or vice versa, or if he had such a business and considers that there are reasons requiring that he should return to Iraq.

(ii) For the purpose of executing the provisions of this Article, the provisions of Article 2 of this Law shall be applied.

Article 5

(a) Any Iraqi Jew who left Iraq after the expiry of Law No. 1 of 1950 or who leaves Iraq or endeavours to leave Iraq illegally after the coming into force of this Law, will forfeit his Iraqi nationality, pursuant to the proposal of the Minister and a decision of the Council of Ministers.

(b) Any Jew who left Iraq with a passport after the coming into force of this Law must return to Iraq within the period to be endorsed in his passport. If he does not return at the termination of the period, the Council of Ministers may, pursuant to the proposal of the Minister, decide to deprive him of his Iraqi nationality, and his property will be disposed of in accordance with Law No. 5 of 1951 and the Regulations which have been issued, or which may be issued, thereunder. The Minister may issue instructions determining the periods for the purpose of the enforcement of this Article.

Article 6

The Minister of Interior should order the deportation of every person deprived of his Iraqi nationality under this Law unless he is convinced, for adequate reasons, that his temporary remaining in Iraq is a matter required by judicial or legal necessity or for safeguarding the officially confirmed rights of third persons.

Article 7

(i) Evidence to prove a claim of ownership of property covered by Law No. 5 of 1951 and this Law will not be accepted unless such evidence is in writing and is countersigned by an official authority before the coming into force of the laws or unless such evidence is based on commercial ledgers drawn up in double-entry style and countersigned by the Notary Public, provided the transaction is entered therein before the coming into force of the law.

(ii) Evidence to prove a claim of a debt against individuals covered by the provisions of the original law and this law will not be accepted unless such evidence is in writing and is countersigned by an official authority before the coming into force of the laws.

(iii) Evidence to prove lease contracts of the property covered by the original law and this law, the terms of which exceed 1 year, will not be accepted except by a Sanad countersigned by an official authority before the coming into force of the laws.

Article 8
The following clause shall be added to the end of Article 1 of Law No. 5 of 1951:

'excepting house furniture, foodstuffs and personal clothing unless the Custodian General decides that they exceed requirements. The Custodian General may exclude trifling articles and sums of money.'

Article 9
This Law shall come into force with effect from the date of its publication in the *Official Gazette*.

Article 10
The Ministers of State are charged with the execution of this Law.

Done at Baghdad this 14th day of Jamad al-Thani 1370 and the 22nd day of March 1951.

FMC
28.3

ABDUL ILLAH
(All Ministers)

Bibliography

Archival Sources

*Public Record Office (*PRO*), London*

1937
Ref. No.   FO 371
20815   Palestine and Transjordan, File No. 22
                         (pp. 5726–864)
20816   Ditto, File No. 22 (pp. 5865–6039)
20817   Ditto, File No. 22 (pp. 6040–245)

1941
Ref. No.   FO 371
27116   Jews in Iraq, File No. 5126

1948
Ref. No.   FO 371
68441–68454   UK-Iraq-Treaty   revision: Political
                         situation in Iraq, File No. 27
68458   Reports on economic conditions in Iraq
                         for March, April, June, October and
                         November 1948, File No. 77
68460–68467   Economic situation in Iraq, File No. 112

68471B	Meeting between the Regent of Iraq and King Abdullah, April 1948, File No. 262
68480	Regulation of religious courts of Christian and Jewish minorities in Iraq, File No. 2021
68481A	Communism in Iraq, File No. 2096
68481B	Iraq: Political Intelligence Reporting, File No. 2096
68641–68644	Efforts of the Arab States to find solutions to the Palestinian problem: proposed Palestine Arab Government: Glubb Pasha's views on disposal of Palestine Arab areas. Union between Transjordan and Arab Palestine, File No. 375

1949

Ref. No.	FO 371
75125	Review of Political events in Iraq in 1948, File No. 1011
75127	Demonstrations in Iraq for more effective prosecution of war in Palestine, File No. 1015
75128	Political situation in Iraq, File No. 1016
75129	Formation of new government, its resignation and formation of new cabinet, File No. 1018
75130	Communism in Iraq, File No. 10110 (pp. to 6818)
75131	Ditto, File No. 10110 (pp. 9504 to end)
75132	Conversation with Iraqi Minister at Cairo on Palestine and situation in the Middle East, File No. 1022.
75133	Iraqi Government reaction to UK de facto recognition of Israel, File No. 1023

75146	Notes for Minister of Defence for his conversation with Regent of Iraq, File No. 1056
75152	Settlement of Palestine refugees in Iraq, File No. 1105
75156	Economic situation in Iraq. Iraq Government's financial difficulties, File No. 1113 (pp. to 2868)
75157	Ditto, File No. 1113 (pp. 3144–9353)
75158	Ditto, File No. 1113 (pp. 9354–12749)
75159	Ditto, File No. 1113 (pp. 12772 to end)
75167	Fears of large-scale Jewish attacks against Iraqi forces. Request for military equipment, File No. 1194
75171	Removal of Iraqi troops from Palestine, File No. 1201
75182	Treatment of Jews in Iraq, File No. 1571 (pp. to 13127)
75183	Ditto, File No. 1571 (13164 to end)
75185	Granting of Iraqi visas to Jews, File No. 1622
75257	Cyprus detainee camps for illegal Jewish immigrants. Release of detainees, File No. 1571
75258	Reports of difficulties with Iron Curtain countries in respect of Jewish immigration into Israel, File No. 1573
75259	Position of Yemen Jews emigrating to Israel via Aden, File No. 1574
75260	Zionist organizations' activities in the United States, File No. 1575
75261	Reports from Israel concerning the immigration of Jews from other parts of the world. Relationship of various Jewish Agencies to each other, File No. 1579

75386	Situation on Iraqi front. Israeli breaches of truce. Israeli ultimatum to King Abdullah for territorial concessions in return for armistice. American attitude. Israel military occupation of part of international zone round Jerusalem, File No. 1095 (pp. to 3850)
75387	Ditto, File No. 1095 (pp. 3852–6816)
75388	Ditto, File No. 1095 (pp. 7022 to end)
75455	Jewish expulsion of non-able-bodied Arabs from Jewish areas of Palestine, File No. 1824

1950

Ref. No.	FO 371
82239	Reactions of various foreign governments to proposals for resettlement and mployment of Palestine Arab refugees, File No. 1823 (pp. to 23)
82477	Ordinance to deprive Jews of Iraq nationality, File No. 1571 (pp. to 6)
82478	Ditto, File No. 1571 (pp. 7–10)
82479	Ditto, File No. 1571 (pp. 11–16)
82480	Ditto, File No. 1571 (pp. 17–20)
82481	Ditto, File No. 1571 (pp. 21–3)
82482	Ditto, File No. 1571 (pp. 24–30)
82483	Ditto, File No. 1571 (pp. 31–41)
82484	Ditto, File No. 1571 (pp. 42–5)
82485	Ditto, File No. 1571 (pp. 46–50)
82486	Ditto, File No. 1571 (pp. 51 to end)
82502	Protection of Iraqi interests abroad, File No. 1931
82505	Social welfare and labour conditions in Iraq, File No. 2181
82506	Annual political report on Israel for 1949, File No. 1011

82512	Treatment of Arabs in Israel, File No. 1018
82538	Economic situation in Israel, File No. 1104
82559	Blocked Arab accounts in Israel, File No. 1154
82618	Immigration into Israel: Knesset passing of Law of Return, declaring right of very Jew to immigrate into Israel; Israeli-Zionist agreement for a joint oordination board, File No. 1574
82619	Proposed exchange of Jewish landowners in Iraq with Arab landowners in srael, File No. 1576

1951

Ref. No.	FO 371
91629	Annual review of events in Iraq during 1950, File No. 1011
91657	Defence policy in Iraqi discussions between General Robertson and Nuri Pasha; proposed stationing of RAF squadrons in Iraq; interview between the Regent of Iraq and the Chief of the Imperial General Staff (CIGS), File No. 1193
91689	Treatment of Jews in Iraq; freezing of assets of Iraqi Jews who left the country; arrangements for transport of Jews from Iraq to Israel, File No. 1571 (pp. to 23)
91690	Ditto, File No. 1571 (pp. 24–47)
91691	Ditto, File No. 1571 (pp. 48–65)
91692	Ditto, File No. 1571 (pp. 66–87)
91693	Ditto, File No. 1571 (pp. 88 to end)

91694	Blocked UK assets of Iraqi Jews residing in Israel; suggested approach by HMG to Iraq to obtain release, File No. 1576
91705	Annual report on Israel for 1950, File No. 1011
91708	Reports on treatment of Arabs in Israel, File No. 1016
91709	Political situation in Israel; general election in July 1951; report on the financial and economic position of Israel; formation of Ben-Gurion's government, File No. 1017 (pp. to 17)
91710	Ditto, File No. 1017 (pp. 18 to end)
91725	Arab balances blocked in Israel; unlocking attempts by Palestine Conciliation Commission not as yet successful, File No. 1153
91751	Jewish immigration into Israel; Israeli Government's attitude to relations with American Jewry, File No. 1571
91752	Emigration of Jews from 'Iron Curtain' countries to Israel, reports of discontent among some of these emigrants, File No. 1573
91797	Iraq-Jordan relations: question of proposed union of the two countries; question of future of Jordan after King Abdullah's death; reactions to new King Talal's approach to Saudi Arabia, File No. 10393 (pp. to 24)

1952
Ref. No.   FO 371

98766	Discussion on route and cost of the Haifa pipeline, question of diversion and throughput of oil, File No. 1535

98767	Treatment of Iraqi Jews; death sentence on two Jews alleged to have attacked Jewish property; trial of twenty-one Jews on charges of belonging to terrorist groups, File No. 1571
98768	Blocking of UK assets of Iraqi Jews resident in Israel, File No. 1572
98769	Request for help in recovering Jewish religious scrolls left behind in Iraq, File No. 1574
98770	Speculation about possible expulsion of all foreign Jews from Iraq, File No. 1575

Iraqi Archives

Directorate of Investigation
Police Folio entitled: 'Anti-Zionist League', No. 41/98
Police Folio entitled: 'The Terrorist Zionists', No. 29/37
Police Folio entitled: 'Papers on the First Central Committee' of the ICP, 7 volumes
Police Folio entitled: 'Papers on the Second Central Committee' of the ICP, 20 volumes
Police Folio entitled: 'Papers on the Third Central Committee' of the ICP, 5 volumes

National Archives
File No. H/216, The arrest of AZL leaders
File No. 10/1923 and 15/1929–1935, Zionist activities in Iraq

Magazines and newspapers
al-Masbah, 1926–1929, M 622
al-Hassid, 1931–1938, H 286
al-Yaqtha, 1944–1952, Y 599
Sada al-Ahali, 1949–1951, S 822
Sawt al-Ahali, 1945–1950

al-Ra'i al-Am, 1944–1950, R 242
al-Iraq, 1945–1952, I 225

Books and Articles

'Abd al-Majid, W. M. (1978): *al-Yahud al-'Arab fi Isra'il: Ihtimalat al-'Awdah wa Ittigahataha* (The Arab Jews in Israel, Prospects for their return), Arabic, Centre for Political and Strategic Studies, al-Ahram, Cairo.

'Abd al-Muhsin, K. (1983): 'The Political Career of Muhammad Ja'far Abu'l-Timman, 1908–1937: A Study in Iraqi History', PhD thesis, School of Oriental and African Studies, London University.

'Abd al-Rahman, A. (1976): 'Awda al-Yahud al-'Arab, al-Mas'ala wa'l-Hull' (The return of Arab Jews, the issue and the solution), Arabic, *Shu'un Falastiniya*, no. 59, August–September 1976.

'Abdo, A. and Kasmieh, K. (1971): *Jews of the Arab Countries*, Palestine Research Centre, Beirut.

Abu Mazin, M. A. (1976): 'Mulahazat hawl Hijra Yahud al-'Iraq' (Notes on the emigration of the Jews of Iraq), Arabic, *al-Talia*, July 1976, Cairo.

Allon. Y. (1970): *The Making of the Israeli Army*, London.

André, J. (1958): 'Death of a Community: Egypt's Vanishing Jewry', *World Jewry*, April 1958.

Ashtor, E. (1976): 'Introduction', in David Corcos: *Studies in the History of the Jews of Morocco*, Rubin Mass, Jerusalem.

Atlas, Y. (1969): *Ad'amud ha-toliyah alilot ha-mahteret be-Iraq* (The Jewish Underground Movement in Iraq), Hebrew, Ma'arakot, Tel-Aviv.

Avidon, Y. (1969): *Alilot Iraq* (Iraqi Activities), Hebrew, Am Oved, Tel-Aviv.

Bar-Moshe, I. (1975): *al-Khuruj min al-'Iraq* (Exodus from Iraq), Arabic, Council of Sephardi Community, Jerusalem.

Barles, H. (1964): *Ha-alia ha-shlishit* (The Third Wave of Immigration), Hebrew, Erez Yahuda, ed., Am Oved, Tel-Aviv.

Bat Ye'or, Y. M. (1974): *The Jews of Egypt*, Sifriat Ma'ariv and the World Jewish Congress.

Batatu, H. (2004): *The Old Social Classes and the Revolutionary Movement in Iraq. A Study of Iraq's Old Landed Commercial Classes and of its Communists, Ba'thists and Free Officers*, Saqi Books, London.

Bein Alex (1970): *Toldot ha-hityaash uut ha-tsiyonit mi-tequfat hertsel we-ad yameinu* (History of the Zionist Colonization), Hebrew, 4th edition, Massada.

Ben-Me'ir, D. (1973): *Mashber ba-h eurah ha-Yisra'elit* (Crisis in Israeli Society), Hebrew, Carta, Jerusalem.

Ben-Ya'acov, A. (1965): *Yehudei Bavel Messof takufat Hagge'onim ad-Yamenu* (A History of the Jews in Iraq, from the End of the Gaonic Period – 1038 CE – to the Present Time), Hebrew, Jerusalem.

Berger, E. (1955): *Who Knows Better Must Say So!*, American Council for Judaism, New York.

Blanc, H. (1964): *Communal Dialects in Baghdad*, Harvard Middle East Monographs, 10, Cambridge, Mass.

Bondy, R. (1978): *The Emissary, A Life of Enzo Sereni*, foreword by Golda Me'ir, Robson Books, London.

Cecil, R. (1941): *The Sassoon Dynasty*, London.

Chouraqui, A. (1968): *A History of the Jews of North Africa*, Philadelphia.

Cohen, H. J. (1966a): 'The Anti-Jewish Farhud in Baghdad, 1941', *Middle Eastern Studies*, vol. 3, October 1966.

—— (1966b): 'A Note of Social Change Among Iraq Jews 1917–1951', *Jewish Journal of Sociology*, vol. VIII, December 1966.

—— (1968): *Ha-Golmin la-aliyah me-artsot asyah we-afriqah be-me ah-ha-esrim* (Twentieth Century Aliyah from Asia and Africa), Hebrew, Hamakhon le-yehadut Zemanru, Jerusalem.

—— (1969): *Ha-pe'ilut ha-tsiyonit be-Iraq* (Zionist Activity in Iraq), Hebrew, Hasifriyah Hatssyonit, Jerusalem. Arabic translation by the Palestine Research Centre, Beirut.

—— (1973): *The Jews of the Middle East, 1860–1972*, Israel University Press, Jerusalem.

—— (1976): *Ha-pe'ilut ha-tsiyonit be-artsot ha-Mizrah ha-tiknon* (Zionist Activity in Countries of the Near East), Hebrew, Ha-Histadrut ha-Tsiyonit, Jerusalem.

Darwish, S. (1981): *Kull Shai' Hadi fi'l-Iyada* (All Quiet in the Clinic), Arabic, Iraqi Graduate League, Jerusalem.

Dayan, M. (1976): *Story of My Life*, Weidenfeld and Nicolson, London.

Divin, R. A. (1952): *American Immigration Policy 1924–1952*, Oxford University Press, London.

Eskandarany, Y. D. (1978): 'Egyptian Jewry, Why it Declined', *Khamsin*, no. 5, 1978.

Eveland, W. G. (1980): *Ropes of Sand. American Failure in the Middle East*, W. W. Norton and Company, London/New York.

Fahmi, A. J. (1952): *Somom al-Afa'a al-Sahyuni* (The Bomb Attacks in Baghdad, Investigation and Trial of the Zionists), Arabic, Matba'at al-Jami'a, Baghdad.

Fischel, W. J. (1937): *Jews in the Economic and Political Life of Medieval Islam*, London.

—— (1944): 'The Jews of Kurdistan. A Hundred Years Ago', Conference on Jewish Relations, New York, 1944, Reprinted from *Jewish Social Studies*, vol. VI, no. 3.

—— (1973) (ed.): *Unknown Jews in Unknown Lands, The Travels of Rabbi David D'beth Hillen (1924–1932)*, Ktav Publishing House, New York.

Furlonge, G. (1969): *Palestine Is My Country, The Story of Musa al-Alami*, John Murray, London.

Gabbay, R. (1978): *Communism and Agrarian Reform in Iraq*, Croom Helm, London.

Gafni, Y. (1975): *Yahadut bavel usmosdoteha* (Babylonian Jewry and its Institutions), Hebrew, Merkaz Shazar Israeli Historical Society.

Gallman, W. J. (1964): *Iraq Under General Nuri, My Recollections of Nuri al-Said 1954–1958*, Johns Hopkins Press, Baltimore.

Ghanima, Y. R. (1924): *Nuzhat al-Mushtaq fi Tarikh Yahud al-Iraq* (History of the Jews of Iraq), Arabic, al-Furat Press, Baghdad.

Ghazzi, O. (1973): 'Al-Awad al-Rahina i'il-Yahud fi Surya' (The Recent Conditions of Syrian Jewry), Arabic, *Shu'un Falastiniya*, no. 19, March 1973.

Gilbert, M. (1976): *The Jews of Arab Lands*, in conjunction with the World Organization of Jews from Arab Countries (WOJAC) and the Board of Deputies of British Jews, Oxford.

Goiten, S. D. (1955): *Jews and Arabs, Their Contacts through the Ages*, Schocken Books, New York.

Grobba, F. (1967): *Männer and Mächte in Orient*, German, Musterschmied Verlag, Zurich.

Gunayim, A. and Abu-Kuf, A. (1969): *al-Yahud wa'l-Harakah al-Sahyuniya fi Misr, 1897–1947* (The Jews and Zionist Movement in Egypt), Arabic, Dar al-Hillal, Cairo.

Ha'am, A. (1947): *Collected Works*, Jewish Publishing House.

Habas, B. (1963): *The Gate Breakers, A Dramatic Chronicle of Jewish Immigration into Palestine*, Herzel Press, New York.

Haim, G. S. (1978): 'Aspects of Jewish Life in Baghdad Under the Monarchy', *Middle Eastern Studies*, vol. 12, May 1978, no. 2.

Hal, L. (1968): 'Israeli Melting Pot', in *World Migration in Modern Times*, Franklin D. Scott, ed., Prentice Hall, Englewood Cliffs, NJ.

Hamidi, J. A. (1976): *al-Tatawwurat al-Siyasa fi'l-'Iraq 1941–1953* (Political Development in Iraq 1941–1953), Arabic, al-Nu'aman Printing House, Najaf, Iraq.

Hasan, M. S. (1965): *al-Tatawwurat al-Iqtisadi fi'l-'Iraq 1954–1958* (Economic Development in Iraq 1954–1958), Arabic, Sidon.

al-Hasani, A. R. (1933–1955): *Tarikh al-Wizarat al-'Iraqiyah* (History of Iraqi Ministries), Arabic, 8 vols., Matba'at al-Irfan, Sidon:
Vol. 1, 1933
Vol. 2, 1934
Vol. 3, 1935
Vol. 4, 1940
Vol. 5, 1953a
Vol. 6, 1953b
Vol. 7, 1955a
Vol. 8, 1955b

—— (1964): *al-Asrar al-Khafiya fi Haraka al-Sana 1941 al-Taharruriya* (The Unrevealed History of the 1941 Liberation Movement), Arabic, Sidon.

Heude, W. (1819): *A Voyage Up the Persian Gulf and a Journey Over Land from India to England*, London.

Hilali, A. (1959): *Tarikh al-Ta'lim fi'l-'Iraq fi'l-'Ahd al-'Uthmani 1638–1918* (History of Education in Iraq Under Ottoman Rule 1638–1918), al-Ahliah Printing House, Baghdad.

Hillel, S. (1977): 'Operation Ezra and Nehemiah', in *Home At Last*, Izriel Eisenberg and Leah Ain Glob, eds., Block Publishing Company, New York.

Hirschberg, H. Z. (1965): *Toldot ha-Yahudim Beffrica ha Tsfonit* (A History of the Jews in North Africa), Hebrew, 2 vols., Bialik Institute, Jerusalem.

Hirst, D. (1977): *The Gun and the Olive Branch*, Faber and Faber, London.

Hourani, A. H. (1947): *Minorities in the Arab World*, Oxford University Press, London.

Husri, S. (1976): *Mudhakkarati fi'l-'Iraq* (My Diary in Iraq), Arabic, Beirut. International Labour Office (1959): *International Migration*, 1954–1957, Geneva.

Itzhaki, A. (1976): 'Hinouch ha-hiudim bi-Iraq bi-me'a ha-eshrim' (Education of Jews of Iraq in the Twentieth Century, Comparative Study), Hebrew, Unpublished Monograph.

Janowski, B. T. (1933): *The Jews and Minority Rights, 1898–1919*, New York.

Julius, I. (1947): *Economics of Migration*, Kegan Paul, Trench, Trubner, London.

Kattan, N. (1976): *Farewell Babylon*, McCleland and Stewart, London.

Kedourie, E. (1970): *The Chatham House Version and Other Middle Eastern Studies*, Weidenfeld and Nicolson, London.

—— (1971): 'The Jews of Baghdad in 1910', *Middle Eastern Studies*, vol. 7, no. 3, October 1971.

Kenwood, A. G. (1971): *The Growth of the International Economy 1820–1960*, Allen and Unwin, London.

Khaddouri, W. (1971): 'The Jews of Iraq During the Nineteenth Century', *Palestine Studies.*

Khadduri, M. (1951): *Independent Iraq: a Study in Iraqi Politics Since 1932*, Oxford University Press, London.

Khairi, S. (1974): *Tarikh al-Haraka al-Thawriya al-Mu'asira fi'l-'Iraq* (History of the Contemporary Revolutionary Movement in Iraq), Arabic, 2 vols, al-Adib Press, Baghdad.

Khalidi, W. (1959): 'Why Did the Palestinians leave?', *Middle East Forum*, XXIV, July 1959.

—— (1971): *From Haven to Conquest*, Institute for Palestine Studies, Beirut.

Khouri, Y. (1970): *al-Yahud fi'l-Buldan al-Arabiya* (Jews in the Arab Countries), Arabic, Dar al-Nahar, Beirut.

Kimche, J. and D. (1976): *The Secret Roads, the Illegal Migration of a People 1939–1948*, Hyperion Press.

Kojman, Y. (1978): *Al-Musiqa al-Funiyah al-Mu'asira fi'l-'Iraq* (Contemporary Art Music of Iraq), Arabic, ACT, London.

Kubbah, M. M. (1965): *Mudhakkarati fi Samim al-Ahdath, 1918–1958*, (My Diary of Iraqi Politics, 1918–1958), Arabic, Dar al-Tali'ah, Beirut.

Landau, M. J. (1969): *Jews in Nineteenth Century Egypt*, New York University Press, New York.

Landshut, S. (1950): *Jewish Communities in the Muslim Countries of the Middle East, a Study*, Jewish Chronicle, London.

Leon, A. (1970): *The Jewish Question: a Marxist Interpretation*, Pathfinder Press, New York.

Lilienthal, A. (1965): *The Other Side of the Coin*, Devin-Adair, New York.

Littman, D. (1976): 'Jews Under Muslim Rule, II, Morocco 1903–1912', *The Weiner Library Bulletin*, vol. XXIX, new series nos. 37/38, Institute of Contemporary History, London.

Loutski, F. B. (undated): *The Modern History of the Arab Countries*, Progress Publishers, Moscow.

Mahkamat al-Sha'b (1959): *Al-Mahkamat* (official account of the conspiracy and corruption trials of the figures of the old regime), Arabic, Ministry of Defence, Baghdad.

Mardor, M. M. (1964): *Strictly Illegal*, foreword by David Ben-Gurion, Robert Hale, London.

Ma'ruf, K. N. (1975): *Al-Aqalliya al-Yahudiya fi'l-'Iraq, 1921–1952* (The Jewish Minority in Iraq 1921–1952), Arabic, 2 vols., al-Dar al-Arabiya, Baghdad.

Massalha, N. (2003): *The Politics of Denial: Israel and the Palestinian Problem*, Pluto Press, London.

Me'ir, Y. (1973): *Me-ever Ha-midbar ha-machteret ha-halutsit be Iraq* (Beyond the Desert, Underground activities in Iraq, 1941–1951), Hebrew, Ministry of Defence, Tel-Aviv; Arabic translation, Centre for Palestine Studies, Baghdad University.

Mizug, G. (1969): *Ye'mei Iyum be-Unevirsitah ha-ivrest bi-Yrushalayim* (Integration of Diasporas in Israel), Hebrew, a symposium held at the Hebrew University, 25–26 October 1966, Magnes Press, Jerusalem.

Morris, B. (1987): *The Birth of the Palestinian Refugee Problem (1947–1949*, Cambridge University Press, Cambridge.

Mu'allim, S. I. (1980): *'Ala Difat al-Furat* (On the Banks of the Euphrates), Arabic, Dar al-Mashriq, Shafa' 'Amr, Israel.

Murad, E. (1977): *Yediday mi Kurdistan* (My Friends from Kurdistan), Hebrew, Yesod, Tel-Aviv.

Nassar, S. (1980): *Al-Yahud al-Masriyun baina'l-Masriya wa'l-Sahyuniya* (The Jews of Egypt: Egyptianism and Zionism), Arabic, Dar al-Wahda, Beirut.

Nur al-Din, M. (undated): *Mudhakkarati 'ala al-Qadiyah al-Falastiniya* (My Diary on Palestine), Arabic, mimeo.

al-Rawi, A. A. (1977): *'Usba Mukafaha al-Sahyuniya* (Anti-Zionist League), Arabic, Centre for Palestine Studies, Baghdad University.

al-Rawi, I. (1969): *Min al-Thawrah al-Arabia al-Kubra ila'l-Iraq al-Hadith* (From the Major Arab Revolution to Modern Iraq), Arabic, Matba'at Dar al-Kutub, Beirut.

Rodinson, M. (1983): 'From the Jewish Nation to the Jewish Problem', comments on A. Leon (1970), in Rodinson, *Cult, Ghetto, and State*, Saqi Books, London.

Sa'd, E. (1969): *Al-Hijra al-Yahudiya ila Falastin* (Jewish Migration to Palestine), Arabic, Palestine Research Centre, Beirut.

Safi, A. R. (1977): *Kifahina didd al-Sihyuniya* (Our Struggle Against Zionism), Arabic, Dar al-Sha'ab, Baghdad.

Said, K. (1966): *Tarikh Harb al-Jaysh al-'Iraqi fi Falastin*, (The War of the Iraqi Army in Palestine), Arabic, Iraqi Army Press, Baghdad.

al-Samarra'i, S.A. (1973): *Muqaddima li Tarikh al-Iraq al-Iqtisadi* (Introduction to Iraqi Economic History, a historical survey of economic development and events in Iraq from the Ottoman Occupation to 1958), Arabic, Najaf.

Sassoon, D.S. (1927): 'History of the Jews in Basra', *Jewish Quarterly Review*, new series, vol. XXII, no. 4, Philadelphia.

—— (1950): *A History of the Jews in Baghdad*, published by his son, Solomon D. Sassoon, The Anguin Press.

Sayyigh, A. (1966): *Al-Hashimiyun wa Qadiya Falastin* (The Hashimites and the Palestine Question), Arabic, al-Maktaba al-Asriyah.

Schechtman, J. B. (1960): *On the Wings of Eagles*, New York.

Schifra, S. (1971): *The Children of Israel, The Bene Israel of Bombay*, Basil Blackwell, Oxford.

Shai, D. (1970): *Neighbourhood Relations in an Immigrant Quarter, a Social-Anthropological Study*, Jerusalem Henrietta Szold Institute, National Institute for Research in Behavioural Science.

Shaloah, A. *et al*, eds. (1976): *Jewish Communities from Central Southern and Eastern Asia in Israel, A Compilation of Data*, Hebrew University, Jerusalem.

Shama, A. (1977): *Immigration Without Integration, Third World Jews in Israel*, Sohenman, Cambridge, Mass.

Shapiro, O. (1971): *Rural Settlements of New Immigrants in Israel*, Rehovot Settlement Study Centre.

Shapiro, R. (1978): 'Zionism and its Oriental Subjects', *Khamsin*, no. 5, 1978, reprinted in *Forbidden Agendas*, Saqi Books, London 1984.

Shenhav, Y. (2002): 'The Phenomenology of Colonialism and the Politics of "Difference": European Zionist Emissaries and Arab-Jews in Colonial Abadan', *Social Identities*, vol. 8, no. 4, 2002, pp. 522–45, Taylor & Francis, Carefax Publishing.

—— (1999): 'The Jews of Iraq, Zionist Ideology, and the Property of the Palestinian Refugees of 1948: An Anomaly of National Accounting', International Journal of Middle East Studies, no. 31, Cambridge University Press, pp. 605–30.

Sicron, M. (1957): *Immigration to Israel 1948–1953*, Statistical Supplement, Falk Project for Economic Research in Israel and Central Bureau of Statistics, Jerusalem.

Slousch, N. (1944): *The Jews in North Africa*, Philadelphia.

Sluglett, P. (1976): *Britain in Iraq 1914–1932*, The Middle East Centre, St Anthony's College, Oxford, Ithaca Press, London.

Stark, F. M. (1945): *East Is West*, John Murray, London.

Stillman, N. A. (1979): *The Jews of Arab Lands, A History and Source Book*, The Jewish Publication Society of America, Philadelphia.

al-Sudani, S. H. (1980): *Al-Nashat al-Sahyuni fi'l-'Iraq, 1914–1952* (Zionist Activities in Iraq, 1914–1952), Arabic, Dar al-Rashid Publications of the Ministry of Culture and Information, Baghdad.

Susa, A. (1978): *Malamih min al-Tarikh al-Qadim li-Yahud al-'Iraq* (The Ancient History of the Iraqi Jews), Arabic, Asa'ad Print House, Baghdad.

Suwaidi, T. (1969): *Mudhakkarati* (My Diary), Arabic, Beirut.

Takriti, S. T. (1978): *Usbat Mukafahat al-Sahyuniya* (Anti-Zionist League), Arabic, Centre for Palestine Studies, Baghdad University.

Taymumi, A. (1982): *Al-Nashat al-Sahyuni fi Tunis, 1897–1948* (Zionist Activities in Tunisia, 1897–1948), Arabic, Tunis.

Thomas, B. (1954): *Migration and Economic Growth*, Cambridge University Press, London.

Twena, A. H., ed. (1975): *Dispersion and Liberation*, vol. 5: *Jewish Education in Baghdad*, Geoula Synagogue Committee, Ramlai.

—— (1977): vol. 6: *The Pogrom in Baghdad.*

—— (1979): vol. 7: *Jewish Autonomy in Iraq.*

'Umari, K. (1978): *Yunis al-Sab'awi, Sirat Siyasi 'Isami* (Yunis al-Sabawi, a Biography of a Self-Made Politician), Arabic, Ministry of Cultural and Art Publications, Baghdad.

al-Wakil, F. H. (1976): *Jama'iya al-Ahali fi'l-'Iraq* (al-Ahali Group in Iraq), Arabic, Dar al-Rashid, Baghdad.

al-Wardi, A. (1976): *Lamhat Ijtima'iya min Tarikh al-'Iraq al-Hadith* (Social Features of the History of Modern Iraq), Arabic, Maktabat al-Ma'arif, Baghdad.

Weizmann, C. (1949): *Trial and Error*, Hamish Hamilton, London.

Wellsted, J. R. (1940): *Travels to the City of Caliphs*, vol. 1, London.

Woolfson, M. (1980): *Prophets in Babylon, Jews in the Arab World*, Faber and Faber, London.

Yasin, A. (1972): 'Usbat Mukafahat al-Sahyuniya fi'l-'Iraq' (Anti-Zionist League in Iraq), Arabic, *Shu'un Falastiniya*, no. 15, November 1972.

Zadok, M. (1966): *Yehudei Teiman* (Jews of Yemen), Hebrew, Va'ad Kehilot, Liw Beyisrael, Tel-Aviv.

Zenner, W. P., ed. (1982): *Jewish Societies in the Middle East: Community, Culture and Authority*, University Press of America, Washington.

Zilkha, Y. H. (1946): *Al-Sahyuniya, 'Aduwa al-'Arab wa'l-Yahud* (Zionism, the Enemy of Arabs and Jews), Arabic, Matba'at al-Hakman, Baghdad.

Index